Lessons from Dad

Lessons from

A Tribute to Fatherhood

Joan Aho Ryan

Health Communications, Inc.
Deerfield Beach, Florida

www.hci-online.com

We would like to acknowledge the following publishers and individuals for permission to reprint the material below. (Note: The items that are in the public domain or were written by Joan Aho Ryan are not included in this listing.)

Papa's Facts of Life and *There Is So Much to Learn*. Reprinted with permission from PAPA, MY FATHER by Leo F. Buscaglia, Ph.D. ©1989 Leo F. Buscaglia, Inc. Published by Slack, Inc.

Duck Hunting. Reprinted by permission of Richard C. Lantzy. ©1997 Richard C. Lantzy.

Learning to Ride. Reprinted by permission of Brian J. Bromberg. ©1997 Brian J. Bromberg.

No Hope on a Rope and *Play It As It Lays*. From FATHERHOOD by Bill Cosby. ©1986 by William H. Cosby, Jr. Used by permission of Doubleday, a division of Bantam Doubleday Dell Publishing Group, Inc.

Cherish the Moment. Reprinted by permission of Harry C. Copeland. ©1997 Harry C. Copeland.

Gilda and Dad: The Show Must Go On. Reprinted from GILDA: AN INTIMATE PORTRAIT by David Saltman ©1992. Used with permission of Contemporary Books, Inc., Chicago.

Even If You Weren't My Father. ©Camillo Sbarbaro. All rights reserved. Translation by Shirley Hazzard; originally published in *The New Yorker*.

She Won't Go to VMI. Reprinted by permission of Art Buchwald. ©1996 Art Buchwald.

(Continued on page 163)

Library of Congress Cataloging-in-Publication Data

Ryan, Joan Aho, date.
   Lessons from dad : a tribute to fatherhood / Joan Aho Ryan.
     p.   cm.
   ISBN 1-55874-479-7 (trade paper)
   1. Father and child—Case studies.   2. Father and child—Anecdotes.
3. Fathers—Case studies.   4. Fathers—Anecdotes.
I. Title.
HQ756.R93   1997   97-7139
306.874'2—dc21   CIP

©1997 Joan Aho Ryan
ISBN 1-55874-479-7

Publisher: Health Communications, Inc.
             3201 S.W. 15th Street
             Deerfield Beach, Florida 33442-8190

Cover design by José Villavicencio

No man can possibly know
what life means, what the world means,
until he has had a child and loves it.
And then the whole universe changes,
and nothing will ever seem exactly
as it seemed before.

—Lafcadio Hearn

Contents

Foreword

Broad social forces over which we have little control are exerting enormous pressures on families today. The obstacles are formidable: the religious, ethnic and cultural diversity of our society; mass media, which influences our children; and the economic pressures that force both mother and father to leave the home for the workplace.

Within the family unit there are the natural pressures of family life—with its moments of joy and disappointment, its Herculean struggles and ordinary routines. Indeed, the story of family life in today's society is one of love striving to overcome a multitude of pressures from within and without.

In coping with these pressures, fathers have come to realize that their involvement in parenting strengthens the family unit and enriches both their children and themselves. Fathers no longer see themselves as merely "providers," but instead are assuming an active role in the care and upbringing of their children. An important aspect of this care is instilling those religious values and practices that become the bedrock of family life.

This is a welcome development, since parenting, especially today, is an act of faith as well as an act of love. To be a parent is to act as God's instrument in giving life to sons and daughters. Equally, parenting is an opportunity for fathers and mothers to be formed by God through their children.

Sometimes children listen and learn; sometimes they teach us. Your wisdom and theirs come from the same Spirit. Fathers and mothers alike should share in this life-affirming experience of parenting as they raise their children in the "church of the home."

Rev. Theodore M. Hesburgh
president emeritus, University of Notre Dame

Acknowledgments

I am indebted to the many people from all walks of life and all parts of the country whose gracious contributions and loving support helped make this book a reality.

I would like to thank Reverend Theodore M. Hesburgh, president emeritus of the University of Notre Dame, for his generosity in writing the foreword for *Lessons from Dad.* This modest endeavor is graced by the words of one of America's foremost spiritual leaders and educators, who reminds us that spiritual values and faith are at the core of good parenting.

I am grateful to the skillful writers who are members of the Lafayette Park Writers Workshop in Tallahassee, Florida. Betsy Bee, Margo Marshall-Olmstead, Dorothy M. Reese and the remarkable Elizabeth Thomson (age 92), whose writing enhanced my first book, *Lessons from Mom,* have once again made their talents available. My thanks to each of them for their friendship and support.

Virginea Dunn Cooper, who has headed the Lafayette Park Writers Workshop for the past 25 years, deserves special recognition for her role in encouraging and orchestrating submissions for the book from many sources. Somehow, she also found time to compose a wonderful tribute to her own father.

My heartfelt thanks go to Joel Kimmel, Mary B. Ledford, Jane Mayes, Margaret A. McDonald, Laurel Turner and Bettie B. Youngs for being part of both collections. I deeply appreciate their willingness to share more "lessons" with all of us.

Throughout this project, my family has given me tremendous support in many ways. My husband, Jack—my partner in life and dearest friend—provided his love, encouragement and excelle⁓ editing skills. I am indebted to our daughter, Diana, for org⁓

and formatting the manuscript of this book. It took great patience and perseverance, considering the mess I had made of things. I would like to thank her for taking on the assignment and for all the other ways she brightens my life.

My mother, who was the inspiration for *Lesson from Mom,* continues to astonish and teach me with her zest for life, and to inspire me with the happiness she gives and receives in loving her family.

To my sister Diane and her husband, Jim, I owe special thanks for their wise counsel, love and understanding at all times. My sister Pat is a constant source of support and encouragement, and I thank her for her love and loyalty.

Peter Vegso and Gary Seidler of Health Communications deserve my thanks for believing in this project and giving me the opportunity to pay homage to fathers everywhere. I am most grateful for the excellent support from their staff as well, particularly my editors, Christine E. Belleris and Mark Colucci, whose editorial judgment was unerringly sound. I am grateful to Mark for the debate he initiated when he knew he was right; he always was. Kim Weiss gave me the benefit of her great public relations talents in launching *Lessons from Dad,* and I appreciate all her efforts.

Finally, thanks to the many people who submitted material for this book: people of all faiths, from coast to coast, from high-school students to retirees. The response was overwhelming, and I regret it was not possible to include every one of the stories, poems and anecdotes sent to me. The number of submissions I received, and the encouragement to produce this book, are gratifying proof that there is no lack of recognition for the loving contribution of Dad, whoever or wherever he may be.

Introduction

Almost 30 years ago, the famed anthropologist Margaret Mead noted the importance of fatherhood during a lecture she delivered at a seminar. Among her remarks was the statement that the emphasis on the mother-child tie in our society may have been appropriate "half a million years ago," at a time "when nobody knew what the father's relationship was. . . . A man came home to a cave for his supper and sex and looked after the children incidentally. . . ."[1]

Nobody would deny that the role of fathers has changed immensely since those days "half a million years ago," and, indeed, since Margaret Mead uttered these words in 1970.

More and more, fathers are helping to care for their children and, in many cases, are the primary caregivers while mothers work outside the home. There has been a widespread and accepted transformation of the traditional roles of mother as caregiver and father as financial provider—the one who returns to the cave at night for food and conjugal pleasures.

It is no longer unusual for mother and father to share equally in the joys and responsibilities of raising their children. As I gathered the pieces for this collection, I was so often struck by the interchangeable roles of parents and the challenges to preconceived notions of what a father's role should be.

---

1. From a transcription of her lecture as quoted in *The Best Parent Is Both Parents: A Guide to Shared Parenting in the 21st Century*, ed. David L. Levy (Norfolk, Va.: Hampton Roads Publishing Co., 1993), p. 9.

The fathers in *Lessons from Dad* are loving, tender and caring. They are remembered fondly by children who waited at the picket fence, or inside an urban high-rise, for a familiar whistle, the aroma of pipe tobacco or a joyous greeting. Some of the stories are from fathers themselves recollecting precious moments of romping with their young children, hearing the first syllables of a baby's attempt at words, or watching with an anxious heart while a son maneuvers his first bicycle or a daughter takes her first steps.

There are many stories, too, about fathers who have no words to express their love, which is felt and remembered decades later. Fathers who were taught it was unmanly to say "I love you" are celebrated in this collection by sons and daughters who "heard" them say it nevertheless, through acts of love and dedication. Their love is remembered in the sharing of a shiny apple, a stern scolding tempered with kindness, a story at bedtime and the various joyful rituals of waiting for Daddy to come home.

What are the other "lessons" from Dad? "Your name is your most valuable possession . . . treat it with respect" is one recalled by many of the contributors to this book. As one father said to his son, "All I have to give you is my good name. Pass it on." This is a powerful message that both sons and daughters thank their fathers for instilling in them.

Bill Cosby, whose tragic loss of his son, Ennis, surely saddened the heart of every parent, has many wise things to say about parenting. The only people who are always sure about how to raise children, he contends, are those who've never had any. I agree. For most of us, parenting is a constant challenge to make the right decisions because we know the stakes are so high, and it's impossible to be right all the time. Still, as this collection illustrates, even fathers who falter and doubt, and who make mistakes they wish they could correct, transmit valuable and lasting positive lessons to their children.

These lessons are the lessons of love. I hope you find much love in these pages and much laughter, too. And whether you're a new dad or a veteran who's grappling with rebellious teens, take comfort in knowing you have a lot of company.

On Your Birthday

Amidst the days of pleasant mirth,
That throw their halo round our earth;
Amidst the tender thoughts that rise
To call bright tears to happy eyes;
Amidst the silken words that move
To syllable the names we love;
There glides no day of gentle bliss
More soothing to the heart than *this!*
No thoughts of fondness e'er appear
More fond, than those I write of here!
No name can e'er on tablet shine,
My Father! more beloved than *thine!*

Elizabeth Barrett Browning
Excerpted from "To My Father on His Birthday"

3

Papa's Facts of Life

*It is not flesh and blood, but the heart
that makes us fathers and sons.*

—Schiller

I have much to thank Papa for. He helped me to grow up more or less sane, a healthy neurotic who laughs a lot, loves a lot, and isn't afraid to cry or be vulnerable. He showed me that life is an exciting adventure and challenged me to take full advantage of all it has to offer. He hooked me on learning and taught me my responsibility for leaving the world a better place for my having been in it.

I'm aware that my life has not been the greatest success story, but, like Papa, I am far from a failure. The facts of life that Papa modeled for me were simple. He lived by a positive code, the rules of which were uncomplicated and accessible to anyone wanting to live a good life:

- Dance, sing and laugh a lot.
- All things are related.
- Don't waste time trying to reason with pain, suffering, life and death.
- An animated person animates the world.
- Find a quiet place for yourself.
- Don't ever betray yourself.

- Birth and death are part of a cycle. Neither begins or ends with you.
- Stay close to your God.
- It's crucial to love.
- Idealism is a strength, not a weakness.
- People are good if you give them a chance to be.
- Discrimination, for any reason, is wrong.
- Self-respect is essential for life.
- Except in the eyes of God, people are not created equal, so we are all responsible for those who can't help themselves.
- Cruelty is a sign of weakness.
- Commitment and caring are the basic ingredients of love.
- Love is indestructible and therefore the most powerful human force.
- Change is inevitable.
- People who think they know it all can be dangerous.

It's true that "everybody gots a father," as the little girl said in the class so many years ago. But there are fathers and there are fathers.

There is always the chance that my deep love for Papa has caused me to be partially blind to his faults. I know he had imperfections, and I am not suggesting that he was a candidate for canonization. But I know for certain that he was very much a selfless person, never dishonest or vindictive.

He was proud, sensitive, affectionate. His greatest fault might have been his obsessive need for security and love—if this is a fault. He was compassionate, naturally intelligent and always concerned about the welfare of others. But no matter what he had or didn't have, was or wasn't, his attitude toward fatherhood made a positive and lasting difference in my life. What else can we ask of another human being?

Thanks, Papa. I'll always love you.

Leo Buscaglia

Duck Hunting

*A person has two legs and
one sense of humor. And if you're
faced with the choice, its
better to lose a leg.*

—Charles Lindner

My first real hunting experience was with my older brother
and my dad in northern Michigan. As a 10-year-old novice, I was
depending on the wealth of knowledge possessed by these two
seasoned vets. Duck hunting is traditionally done in less-than-
ideal weather, so the morning began perfectly with a fine, freezing mist that greeted us at the beaver dam near our cabin.

Dad was always in complete control because he was the only
one who knew what he was doing. My brother didn't always
agree, even though my dad often reminded him. So when it was
time to place the decoys, Dad had to take over that process from
my brother for obvious reasons. "You're not getting them out far
enough," said Dad, as he took the decoys. "I'll have to do it
myself." When you know what you're doing, even an ice-covered
log is no deterrent—especially if the job is to be done right.

As Dad worked his way along the log, he reminded us again
that the decoys had to be as far out as possible. His first decoy
toss was his last for the day. To me it looked like he had forgotten
to let go as he followed the decoy from the icy log into the beaver

dam. The water appeared to be only inches deep, but when this six-foot man in waders and a heavy hunting jacket disappeared into the muck below, my brother did not hesitate. Within seconds, my father was being pulled from the muck, coughing and gasping for air.

My brother had saved his life, but, of course, the incident would not have happened if he would have thrown the decoys into the pond the right way. In my dad's anger, fear and embarrassment, we were the targets of his ire—perhaps because we thought the whole thing was funny. We were told to collect the decoys and walk back to the cabin since he had to get back and dry off. I guess even when a tyrant yells at you, it's funny if he's covered with muck. Each laugh of ours made him angrier. When he took out his pack of cigarettes for a smoke, it was full of muck. Naturally, we laughed even harder. When he took off his glasses to flick off the mud and hit his hand against the tree, we knew we were in real trouble. We were still roaring when Dad slammed the car door and drove off into the woods. It was only a mile or so to the cabin, and we enjoyed the time to relive the scene many times over on our way back.

Trying as hard as we could to stop laughing, we put off facing Dad as long possible. Dad had gone outside. When we thought we had ourselves under control, we opened the door to the cabin. An indescribable stench literally took our breath away. There was Dad sitting at the table in his long underwear smiling. "Really stinks, huh?" he said, grinning.

We spent the rest of the afternoon reliving the hunting "accident," and all three of us laughed together for the first time I could remember.

My dad never expressed in words his thanks to my brother for saving his life, but he truly had a different attitude about doing things his way from then on. The incident seemed to have given us all a better perspective about dealing with others. Dad seemed to be much more tolerant with us, and my brother and I have enjoyed being with him much more since we almost lost him.

Although I never went duck hunting again, the three of us can still chuckle about that day at the beaver dam some 40 years ago.

No matter how many times we tell the story, it seems Dad laughs
the loudest. Among all the valuable facts of life I have gained
from my father, I cherish my sense of humor the most.

Richard C. Lantzy

Learning to Ride

His heritage to his children wasn't words or possessions, but an unspoken treasure, the treasure of his example as a man and as a father. More than anything I have, I'm trying to pass that on to my children.

—Will Rogers Jr.

The morning of my birthday, I awoke at 7:30 to a glorious surprise. Although the sun's first rays brought a little light through my window, most of my room remained in shadow. Through the dim light, my unfocused eyes made out the silhouette of a new bicycle standing in front of my dresser. I leapt out of bed and almost tripped over my own feet as I rushed for the light switch.

As the pale light illuminated the room, I realized my birthday wish had come true: my parents had bought me a Schwinn bicycle. Immediately, I named my prized possession *Bobby Schwinn,* for I wanted to be on a first-name basis with my new best friend. I knew right away I would love and care for this bike. All I had to do was learn how to ride it.

I ran into my dad's room to demand bike-riding lessons.

"You know, Brian, I can put training wheels on it for you," he said.

"Training wheels are for girls!" I protested.

Dad evidently agreed that there are serious differences in how

9

boys and girls approach bike riding. He said he'd teach me to ride that day, without the benefit of training wheels.

When the afternoon finally arrived, I went out into the street with my father and Bobby Schwinn, intent on becoming the best bicycle rider in the world. Dad showed me how to raise the kickstand and helped me sit upright on the uncomfortable seat. As I wobbled back and forth, he held the back of the seat with one hand and the handlebars with the other.

"Relax," Dad said, "and hold steady."

Then he began to run, pushing the bicycle along the road. I was assured that he would hold on tight as I repeatedly yelled "don't let go," while we flew down the street. When I became satisfied that Dad was holding the bike securely, I gathered up enough confidence to actually enjoy myself. I felt the wind in my face and the proud smile of my mother from the driveway. My dad ran with me down to the stop sign at the end of the street, then turned and ran back to the house, guiding the bicycle all the way.

"You want to try it by yourself now, Brian?" Dad asked.

"No," I said. "Let's do it again together."

Dad sighed. I imagine he was not thrilled at the idea of running down the hot street again. But he did, as I struggled to hold the handlebars straight, pedal faster and keep my balance at the same time.

"Let's go faster," I called back to Dad, but he did not answer. Glancing over my shoulder, I noticed that Dad had stopped running and was standing a few feet behind me, watching me steer the bike all by myself. I faltered, suddenly aware that I could not control this contraption by myself. Wobbling madly, I struggled to avoid falling to the hard pavement below. I hoped for the best, but lost control. The handlebars veered to the left, and I collided with our brown Dodge, which was parked at the curb.

I yelped as Bobby Schwinn hit the car and threw me off his back onto the hard asphalt. I cried as I got up and kicked Bobby Schwinn as hard as I could. That was it! I would never get on a bike again.

I started to walk back to the house, upset at my failed attempt and my smashed birthday present. Dad ran over to me with a

smile on his face. I didn't see what was so funny. I could have
been really hurt.

"Where are you going?" Dad asked.

"Inside," I yelled. "I hate that stupid bike. I can't ride it!"

Dad knelt down and dried my eyes.

"Never say 'can't'," Dad said. "You *can* do it. You can do anything you want. It just takes time. Learning to ride a bike doesn't
come naturally. You have to work at it. So you hit the car. The
car's fine, the bike's fine."

He looked me over. "You look okay, too. Any broken bones?
Any cuts or scrapes?" Seizing the opportunity for a little pity, I
pointed to a dirty elbow. Dad just laughed, and I couldn't help
but join in.

"Son, you're not always going to succeed at everything right
away," he said. "But you don't just try it once. If you want something, you have to work for it. You can't let one little fall scare
you away."

Scare? Dad had used the magic word. That was like being chicken,
and no self-respecting boy would stand for that. So I tried again.

I crashed into the mailbox, the stop sign, the tree that someone had planted too close to the road and a pedestrian walking
his dog. Through it all, Dad made me get back on the bike. By
the day's end, I had tamed Bobby Schwinn.

I don't recall Dad allowing any obstacles to get in his way. He
always went for what he wanted—and usually got it. To this day,
Dad's lessons about not giving up are with me: when I went into
physical therapy after a partially paralyzing stroke; when I doubted
that my mediocre grades would get me into the University of
Florida (I got in); and when my short stories, poems and novels
met with rejection, I remembered Dad and Bobby Schwinn.

Thanks to Dad I know that no matter how hard the task is or
what obstacles are in the way, I have to keep getting back on that
bike.

Brian J. Bromberg

No Hope on a Rope

In this world, there are only two tragedies.
One is not getting what one wants,
and the other is getting it.

—Oscar Wilde

I am happy most of the time. Except on Father's Day. I am never as happy as I deserve to be on Father's Day. The problem is my presents. I trust my family to get them instead of simply buying them for myself; and so, I get soap-on-a-rope.

In the entire history of civilization, no little boy or girl ever wished on a star for soap-on-a-rope. It is not the dumbest present you can get, but it is certainly second to a thousand yards of dental floss. Have you ever tried to wash your feet with soap-on-a-rope? You could end up with a sudsy hanging.

Of course, soap-on-a-rope is not the *only* gift that can depress a father on Father's Day: there are many others, like hedge cutters, weed trimmers and plumbing snakes. It is time that the families of America realized that a father on Father's Day does not want to be pointed in the direction of manual labor.

We could also do without a 97th tie or another pair of socks, and we do not want a sweater in June. We appreciate the sentiment behind the buying of a sweater—it was on sale—but we still would rather have a Corvette.

Mothers do not permit Mother's Day to be run like this. Even

General Patton would have lacked the courage to give his mother soap-on-a-rope. Mothers, in fact, organize the day as precisely as Patton planned an attack. They make a list of things they want, summon their children and say, "Go see your father, get some money from him and surprise me with some of these."

The kids then go to the father and say, "Dad, we need $8,000 for some presents for Mom."

Mothers stress the lovely meaning of Mother's Day by gathering their children and tenderly saying, "I carried every one of you in my body for nine months, and then my hips started spreading because of you. I wasn't built like this until you were born, and I didn't have this big blue vein on the back of my leg. *You* did this to me."

For Father's Day, however, this woman comes to you and says, "It's one of those compulsory holidays again, one of those meaningless greeting-card things, so the kids are under pressure to buy some presents for you and the money is certainly not coming from *me*. Twenty bucks for each of them should do it—unless you'd rather have me put it on your charge."

You have five children, so you give her $100. The kids then go to the store and get two packages of underwear, each of which costs five dollars and contains three shorts. They tear them open and each kid wraps one pair of shorts for me. (The sixth pair is saved for a Salvation Army drive.) Therefore, on this Father's Day, I will be walking around in new underwear, and my kids will be walking around with $90 change.

Not every year, of course, do I get Old Spice or underwear. Many times a few of my kids are away from home on this special day, but they always remember to call me collect, thus allowing the operator to join in the Father's Day wishes, too. I have, in fact, received so many of these calls that I'm thinking of getting an 800 number.

On Father's Day, which is almost as exciting as Groundhog Day, I sometimes think of a famous writer named Dorothy Parker, who said that men were always giving her one perfect rose but never one perfect limousine. Well, I understand just how she felt. For just *one* Father's Day, I would like the kids to forget about the underpants, the tie and the tin trophy saying *World's Greatest*

Father and instead surprise me with a Mercedes. Just put $200 down on it, and I'll gladly finish the payments.

It will never happen, of course, because fathers are good actors who lie well. A father can sound convincing when he says that he is delighted to have another bottle of Old Spice because he is down to his last six. A mother, however, will refuse to accept such a bottle or a little tin trophy and will send the children back to the store to get it right. After all, it's the thought that counts. And did you kids think she was *crazy?*

On every day of the year, both mothers and fathers *should* be given more recognition than a jock or a trophy. I am still waiting for some performer to win an award and then step to the microphone and say, "I would like to thank my mother and father, first of all, for letting me live."

Bill Cosby

Cherish the Moment

Nothing is worth more
than this day.

—Goethe

"It's not whether you are catching any fish, Son, it's being out there and enjoying the moment that counts."

These words, spoken to a very bored adolescent in the early 1940s, have echoed through my mind for half a century. They have reminded me on many occasions that we should cherish every fleeting moment.

My dad, an avid fisherman, took advantage of every hour away from work. He'd hitch up the family boat, with his prized Johnson outboard motor, to the trailer. Then he would load it with fishing poles, rods, reels and bait—from wriggling earthworms to sticky catalpas. He always took plenty of snacks for us as we headed for one of his favorite fishing meccas: the Dead Lakes in Florida's Panhandle.

On these mythic outings, I usually brought along some Ellery Queen or Perry Mason mysteries, a World War II adventure, a Zane Grey western or one of the popular Hardy Boys novels. (Dad had bought me the whole Hardy Boys adventure mystery set—more than 20 titles in all—for 49¢ each.)

On the day Dad gave me his unforgotten advice—as we waited fruitlessly for a shellcracker or bream or bass to take our hooks—

I longed for some cool, shady spot back at the landing with one of my treasured books. In those restless childhood years, the books were my escape, along with movies about action heroes.

Miserable from the fatiguing heat, the annoying gnats and the hard boat seat, I remarked to Dad that I was bored with the lack of action from beneath the waters. "It's not whether you are catching any fish, Son," he said. "It's being out there and enjoying the moment that counts." At the time, it did not relieve my discontent. Yet, curiously, it has worked enchantment into all of life's challenges.

Dad's lesson was: wherever you are or whatever you're doing, cherish the moment. Life is too short not to savor the nectar and ambrosia that can be found in each situation. Over the years, when I found myself in danger of becoming disenchanted with what life dished out, I recalled my dad's comment on that now misty day on the Dead Lakes. Those words transformed my outlook and awoke within me a fire that has helped me reach out to others.

Dad taught me two other valuable lessons: responsibility and love for other creatures.

We usually had dogs, cats, goats, chickens, rabbits and other four-legged animals. Dad reserved particular love for a beautiful, glossy-haired female English setter named Belle that was his constant companion.

In raising and training Belle, Dad showed me the importance of responsibility; in caring for and nurturing her, he revealed the quality of love. When she died of poisoning, he was devastated.

This lesson in responsibility and love carried over into caring for my pony Nellie. What wonderful excursions we took in my small, rural hometown of Marianna, Florida. But I quickly learned that it wasn't all enchantment. There were tasks: feeding her, keeping the saddle and blanket clean, currying her, brushing her mane, and suffering the excruciating pain when she stepped on my bare foot!

In moments of boredom, pain, uncertainty or fear, I remember the words Dad spoke to me that hot, miserable day. Throughout my life, the words *cherish the moment* have sustained me.

Harry C. Copeland

Gilda and Dad:
The Show Must Go On

Hope for the best. Expect the worst.
Life is a play. We're unrehearsed.

—Mel Brooks

One of Gilda's [Gilda Radner's] favorite pictures was taken when she was eight years old, at her brother's bar mitzvah in Detroit. Gilda, glassy-eyed, is dancing with her father. She is wearing a dark satin dress and petticoats; he is wearing black tie and looking as blissful as she.

She and Herman loved to go to the theater together in downtown Detroit. They would always sit in the third row, and Gilda was certain all the performers were looking directly at her. Years later, when she herself was performing on Broadway, she was stunned to find that when she looked out into the audience she was blinded by the lights and could not see a thing.

Gilda's father took her to her first Broadway productions at the old Riviera Theater; together they saw road shows of *Li'l Abner, Most Happy Fella* and even *Rigoletto.* It was after one of these productions that Herman confided to his only daughter that he had never really wanted to become a business and real estate tycoon. His dream had always been to work as a song-and-dance man in the theater.

"He could have done it, too," Gilda said often.

17

"Some of his spunk must have come out in me because he used to love to perform. He was funny. He was a good storyteller. He did magic tricks. He loved to sing, and he could tap-dance, and he couldn't carry a tray of food to the table without tripping to make us kids laugh and make my mother nervous. In the years that I've been performing I feel that some part of my father is back alive in me, back doing what he always wanted to do."

Her father loved corny jokes, and he used to love to watch her perform, calling her "my little ham" to alternate with "my heart."

Her father's dream became her dream as well. His nightmare also became hers.

"He had been having headaches for a couple of years. But really, there was no warning. He thought it was his glasses. It happened out of the clear blue. He suddenly developed brain cancer when I was 12. One day—boom, it hit him. He went into the hospital for some routine tests, and really, as far as I was concerned, he never came out. At first, whenever he saw me, he would begin to cry. And then he just lay there like a vegetable for two years, terminally ill. His tumor was too far gone to remove. And then he died when I was 14 years old," she said sadly, "and left a scrapbook of newspaper clippings. . . .

"He was the love of my life," Gilda said simply, sitting there at that big white table, with just a trace of a tear in her eye.

Gilda was away at summer camp the day he died. On August 10, 1960, in the early morning, she was sound asleep when the camp owner woke her up, saying her mother had called, her father had "taken a turn for the worse," and she should go home. She flew back to Detroit in a small plane. Her brother met her at the airport, and he did something he had never done before: he took her hand. Suddenly Gilda knew her father was dead.

In accord with the Jewish tradition, she sat *shiva* for a week, trying to pray for her father's soul, as relatives, friends and well-wishers visited the house in an unending stream, all bringing food. After the week of *shiva,* still numb with shock, at her request Gilda returned to camp. She had rehearsed her part as Bloody Mary in the camp production of *South Pacific,* and she knew that her father would have said "The show must go on!"

David Saltman

Even If You Weren't
My Father

Father, even if you weren't my father,
were you an utter stranger,
for your own self I'd love you.
Remembering how you saw, one winter morning,
the first violet on the wall across the way,
and with what joy you shared the revelation;
then, hoisting the ladder to your shoulder,
out you went and propped it to the wall.
We, your children, stood watching at the window.

And I remember how, another time,
you chased my little sister through the house
(pigheadedly, she'd done I know not what).
But when she, run to earth, shrieked out in fear,
your heart misgave you,
for you saw yourself hunt down your helpless child.
Relenting then, you took her in your arms
in all her terror: caressing her, enclosed in your embrace
as in some shelter from that brute
who'd been, one moment since, yourself.

Father, even were you not my father,
were you some utter stranger,
for your innocence, your artless tender heart
I would above all other men
so love you.

Camillo Sbarbaro
translated from the Italian by Shirley Hazzard

She Won't Go to VMI

*It is impossible to please all the world
and also one's father.*

—La Fontaine

As soon as the Virginia Military Institute voted to accept women at the school, a version of the following scene took place among alumni all over the state.

"Alice, I have good news for you. You can now enroll in VMI, my alma mater."

"Daddy, I don't want to go to VMI. I want to go to Radcliffe."

"Shame on you! Radcliffe is for girls."

"But I *am* a girl."

"VMI will give you the steel and discipline that your brother and I have. I have dreamed of this moment for years. The fact that you can now enroll is an opportunity you can bless the Supreme Court for."

"Dad, I read that they'll shave the heads of the women cadets to teach them a lesson."

"You won't be sorry. One day when you're in the trenches of Malaysia, you will thank VMI for shaving your head. You will also understand that they had to shave your head to wash your brains."

"Daddy, I really don't want to spend my college years doing push-ups."

"Bite your tongue! Everyone has to do push-ups. You can't fire missiles at the Iraqis if you are unable to flex your muscles. VMI is perfect for you."

"If I can't go to Radcliffe, can I go to Smith?"

"They don't teach you character at Smith. VMI is the only institution where they instruct you on how to throw yourself on a live hand grenade and win the Medal of Honor."

"I was hoping to become an interior decorator, not a war hero."

"I'd hate to see you waste your life drawing pictures of living rooms when you could be on a 29-mile hike with only one canteen of water and cold C-rations."

"Daddy, I appreciate your wanting me to attend your alma mater, but I am not a chip off the old block. I believe in the military, but not as a career for me."

"But I've already sent off your application. I get special treatment because I was in the top 10 percent of my class. I can't cancel the application."

"I'm not going. I am not interested in carrying a rifle around and eating VMI food. I don't want to prove that I'm better than a man when it comes to running the obstacle course, nor do I want male cadets chewing me out because my shoes aren't shined."

"I never thought that a daughter of mine would reject the opportunity to learn how to deal with mental pressure, physical stress and psychological bonding. You've let me down."

"Sorry, Pops, but maybe you can come visit me if I go to Sweet Briar."

"Doesn't any young Southern woman care about going to Somalia any more?"

Art Buchwald

A Phone Call to Father

If you are able to say how much
you love, you love little.

—Petrarch

It was a typical June day in San Francisco, cool and overcast. Reading the newspaper, I noticed the East Coast was suffering a heat wave and Father's Day was approaching. Father's Day, like Mother's Day, never meant much to me. I've generally regarded those days as good for merchants and convenient for children.

Putting down the paper, I looked up at a photograph of Father on my desk. My sister had taken it several summers ago in Beddeford Pool, Maine. Father and I stood together on the porch of a cottage, our arms around each other's shoulders. By the looks of us the apple didn't fall far from the tree. I thought about calling to see how he and Mother were doing.

I picked up the photograph and examined it closely. That was my old man, no doubt about it. With his top teeth out, he grinned like a grizzled ex-hockey player. His eyes were set deep in a sun-creased face; he had a cocky stance even at 70 years old. I could smell his Lucky Strikes, Scotch and bay rum.

It was a younger man who once chased me along the beach and took me into the water; a stronger man who taught me how to row, skate and split firewood. That was before his plastic knee, false teeth and hearing aid. I decided to give the old man a call.

"Good afternoon," he shouted. Mother picked up the other phone and told him to put his hearing aid in.

"I've got it here in my pocket," he said, and I heard him fumbling for it.

Mother said the air conditioning was a godsend, her plastic hip was all right and the new dog was driving her nuts.

"Actually," she said, "it's not the dog, it's your father."

"What's the matter?" I asked.

"Shep can jump over the fence, and he does whenever the mood strikes him. Then he takes off to God knows where. Your father worries about Shep and waits up until he comes back. He's out there at two in the morning, calling the dog and making an awful racket. Then when Shep comes back, he scolds him—'Malo perro, malo, malo'—as if we were back in Peru and the dog understood Spanish."

"I think he's learning," said Father, back on the line. "Your mother thinks I'm a damn fool, and she's probably right."

"You're still shouting," said Mother.

He ignored her and asked me how I was doing. I told him.

"Freelancing is fine," he said loudly, "but you need security. You're too old to be cooking on yachts, tending bar and working construction. You've got a college education, why don't you use it? What are you going to do if you get sick? You know how much it costs to stay in a hospital?"

"You know," I told him, "I can't figure you out. You smoke too much, drink too much, don't exercise, eat all the wrong foods, and you're still a tough old goat."

"You're right," he said. "And I'm outliving all my classmates." He said it without bragging.

There was something I wanted to tell the old man, and I was having a difficult time getting it out.

"Do you read the newspaper clippings I send you?" he asked.

"Sure, I do."

"I don't know whether you do or not—you never write."

I wasn't forgetting that he and I had had our differences over the past 44 years and that we had angered, disappointed and cursed each other often. But those times seemed long ago, and I wanted to tell him I loved him. I wanted to be funny, and I wanted the telephone call to flow.

"Listen," I told him, "I understand Father's Day is coming up." "Oh," he said, uninterested. He never kept track.

"It's the 17th," said Mother on the other phone.

"I'm sorry I jumped through the top of your Lincoln convertible," I said.

"You were six," he said and chuckled. "I couldn't believe it at first."

I wanted to thank him for the hockey games, chess games, books and lobster dinners. I wanted to apologize for punching him in the eye when I was 18.

"Thanks for being my father," I said.

He was quiet on his end, and Mother, too. A long-distance microstatic filled the void.

"I wish I'd been better," he said, his voice subdued for the first time.

"You were just fine," I said. "A guy couldn't have had a better father."

"Good of you to say, old boy, but not true. I wish it were," he said, with regret in his voice.

"It is true," I hurried on. "Do you remember when I wanted to feed sugar to the donkey at the cricket club and you patted him on the rump, and he kicked you?"

"Yes," chuckled Father. "Smashed my knee, damn beast. You always thought that was funny."

"And all those ships you took me aboard," I added.

"There were a few of those," he conceded. "Boy, you're really taking me back."

"I loved the ships," I told him.

"But still I couldn't convince you to go in the navy."

"I wanted you to go to college after high school," said Mother.

"But you wouldn't listen," said Father. "You had to be a marine."

I didn't say anything. I heard them remembering.

"And we flew out to California," continued Father, "to say good-bye before you left for Vietnam."

"We stayed at the Newporter Inn," said Mother, "and went to Disneyland."

Father continued, "I had to leave that Sunday night by helicopter to catch a flight out of Los Angeles. Your mother and the girls stayed in the hotel, and you walked me to the helipad. You were in uniform, and we shook hands. . . ." His voice trailed off.

"I didn't know if I'd ever see you again," he said. "I cried on that helicopter. It tore me up, your leaving."

"I know," I said, feeling a lump in my throat.

"We prayed for you," he said, his voice beginning to tremble. "We lived for your letters."

"And I for yours," I told him. This was crazy, I thought. My eyes were damp, and I swallowed to clear the lump.

"I called to wish you a happy Father's Day," I managed to say.

"That was good of you, old boy. I'll hang up now; don't want to run up your bill." His voice was shaking.

"Don't worry about the bill," I said. "I love you."

"I love you, too. Good-bye and God bless you," he said hurriedly and hung up.

"You know how he gets," said Mother quietly.

"I know," I said, and after another minute we hung up.

I looked at the photograph of Father and me on the porch in Maine. Yes, I thought, I know how he gets. I wiped my eyes, smiled at the picture and blew my nose loudly. The apple didn't fall far from the tree.

George Eyre Masters

Independence for Marlo

*One of the things about equality is
not just that you be treated equally to a man,
but that you treat yourself equally to
the way you treat a man.*

—Marlo Thomas

My kids were growing up, and Marlo, of course, was the first to attend USC. She had done very well scholastically at Marymount High School and easily was admitted to this hard-to-get-into university. She still lived at home. In my Lebanese tradition, a daughter doesn't leave unless she's wearing a white veil and a ring on her finger. Rosie, in particular, played hardball in this matter.

So Marlo commuted to college every day, driving about 15 miles each way in Los Angeles's crazy freeway traffic. She was a brilliant student, ending up with a 3.8 average. She was seriously planning to be a teacher and, in fact, spent many months—as part of a USC educational project—working as a teaching assistant in the barrio schools of East Los Angeles. Very few people know that about Marlo.

From day one, I had tried to talk her out of an acting career. I told her I didn't want her to have to suffer the heartbreak and rejection I had seen so many times with young women trying to make a go of it in my profession. And when Marlo seemed so enthusiastic about teaching, I thought I was succeeding. Little did I know. After all, she was carrying my genes.

Marlo tried out for dramatic productions at USC and was cast in some of them. Rosie and I went to see her and she was quite good. But I kept up my drumbeat of what I call "hairy stories" about the perils of show business, and she seemed to be listening. She was listening all right, but she had inherited another genetic characteristic from me—stubbornness.

On the day we came home from her commencement, Marlo steered me into my office at home. She threw her diploma down on my desk and said, "This is for *you*. Now, how do I become an actress?" What's a father to do? I told her that if that's what she really wanted, I'd do all I could to give her the proper advice.

But that was only the first of a double-barreled shot. Marlo said, "Dad, I want to leave home and go out on my own. I don't even know how to open a can of sardines. I've been too sheltered and protected. I've got to become more independent. What if, heaven forbid, something should happen to you and Mommy, where would I be? You've got to talk to Mom about letting me go."

That's when I first began to call Marlo "Miss Independence." And it didn't surprise me at all when she later turned out to be one of the foremost advocates of women's rights.

Danny Thomas
with Bill Davidson

She Never Looked Back

*This above all: to thine own self be true,
And it must follow, as the night the day,
Thou canst not then be false to any man.*

—Hamlet
Polonius's advice to his son

It was summertime, 1984. Jenny would soon be seven years old. I lay abed reading. Jenny came softly into my room, checking to see if I was awake and, if so, good for any games. She stood beside the bed, eyes dancing, full of some new idea, some scheme; I would know soon enough.

I looked up at her. "Hi, Daughter. I sure do like you."

"I like you, too," she said, and sat at the edge of the bed. I tousled her thick wavy hair; she smiled and said, "Dad, what's it like to see the sunrise?"

"Beautiful. Best time of day. The whole world is quiet and still. Fools are not up yet. There are never any two sunrises alike. There are sunrises of gold and purple splendor beneath the clouds. There are clear and brilliant sunrises, and on a dark and cloudy day no sunrise at all."

"What's it like on a cloudy day?"

"You just become aware that the night is passing. Things get easier to see, lighter shades of gray. Why do you ask?"

"Oh, just giving you some material for the book."

29

The book, I decided, was over. I had been waiting for some kind of a sign, anyway.

Did I miss anything in the telling? How about the time when she was five and came in, all serious and sober, sat beside me and asked me to tell her the most important thing she'd need to know for when she was grown up. I said, "Come back in 10 minutes." Ten minutes of serious thought and soul searching. She was back, and I was satisfied I had found a worthy answer for her.

"Two things, Daughter, both easy to remember. The first is from the Bible. It is so short, so simple, the we have come to call it the Golden Rule. Here it is: 'Do unto others as you would have them do unto you.'

"The second is from Shakespeare, who was a great English writer. He lived a long time ago, but many of the things he wrote are as true today as they were then. In a play called *Hamlet,* Shakespeare wrote, 'This above all: to thine own self be true.'"

Jenny was silent a moment, nodded sagely, then she was gone. Off to something else.

"How'd I do?" I asked Diane, who had been listening from her end of the couch. She made no comment. I went on. "What a remarkable person we are sending into the 21st century. What happened to women like her in the Victorian age, and even before that?" Sure bait for Diane, I knew.

She was quick to reply. "They were taught out of the Bible and by every other means to be submissive. That men were superior to women."

"What a waste of humanity," I said.

"Do you realize how far you have come in your thinking?" asked Diane. Then, with a little grin and in exactly the same tone of voice she uses to talk to the half-witted tomcat Keats, she said, "Come here, and I'll give you a pat on the head."

I had started for her when the phone rang.

"I'll get it," called Jenny. Then, "It's Joyce. Can I go over to her house and play?"

"I'll walk you to the corner," I called back. That was our agreement. Joyce lived less than two blocks away, her house in view from the corner across a through street.

"Don't cross the street with me, Dad. Let me go on alone from here."

I stood and watched her look both ways, then run to her little friend's house. Through sun and shadow, light glinting on her hair. So strong. So eager.

She never looked back. She doesn't need to look back anymore. I don't know why I felt that so sharply. Daddies raise daughters only to give them away. But I dread my growing old and dying, and I am so flawed, and time is running out so fast. With Jenny I can go in peace. For I would rather leave Jenny on this earth than the Pyramids.

Gordon Baxter

Play It As It Lays

*One learns in life
to keep silent and draw one's
own confusions.*

—Cornelia Otis Skinner

It is no profound revelation to say that fathering has changed greatly from the days when my own father used me for batting practice. However, the baffling behavior of children is exactly the same today as it was when one of Joseph's brothers peddled him to the Egyptians. And in the face of such constantly baffling behavior, many men have wondered: just what *is* a father's role today?

The answer, of course, is that no matter how hopeless or cope-less a father may be, his role is simply to *be* there, sharing all the chores with his wife. Let her *have* the babies; but after that, try to share every job around. Any man today who returns from work, sinks into a chair and calls for his pipe is a man with an appetite for danger. Actually, changing a diaper takes much less time than waxing a car. A car doesn't spit on your pants, of course, but a baby's book value is considerably higher.

If the new American father feels bewildered and even defeated, let him take comfort from the fact that whatever he does in any fathering situation has a 50 percent chance of being right. Having five children has taught me a truth as cosmic as any that you can find on a mountain in Tibet: there are no absolutes in raising children. In any stressful situation, fathering is always a roll of the dice. The game may be messy, but I have never found one with more rewards and joys.

You know the only people who are *always* sure about the proper way to raise children? Those who've never had any.

Bill Cosby

A Man of Many Faces

The following is excerpted from a speech given before the National Father's Day Committee on May 25, 1961.

It is an all too visible truth that fatherhood is no longer the sacred duty it was once held to be. There are, today, far too many absentee fathers, fathers in name only. Paradoxically—and this is an insight into the nature of contemporary society—they are, in many cases, men whose ability, sense of responsibility and moral integrity outside the home are of the first order.

Apologists for these errant progenitors (in most instances, offenders themselves) have called up a multitude of rationalizations in their defense—two world wars in less than half a century, the pressures of modern urban life, business before pleasure, country before self and other tired old saws.

What nonsense. There is absolutely no excuse for a parent to abdicate his most important duty—the proper raising of his children. No father should be allowed to get away with the cowardly logic which concludes that his only job in the family is to pay for the bacon.

His role is much more grandiose than that. If it is to be properly fulfilled, he should be, in his realm, a man of many faces—an artist, a philosopher, a statesman and, above all, a prolific dispenser of good sense and justice.

But it is vitally important, especially in the early years, that his children see in Father a working model of the social order in which, not so many years hence, they will be expected to play a dynamic part.

How can we, the parents, hope to secure a just and rational society if we neglect the development of those very instruments, our children, most necessary for its implementation? What good does it do to conceive grand moral, social or political plans for a better world if the children who will have to live them out fail to see their importance?

Adlai E. Stevenson

Country Smart

*I just owe almost everything to
my father, [and] it's passionately interesting for
me that the things that I learned in a small town,
in a very modest home, are just the things
that I believe have won the election.*

—Margaret Thatcher

When Ralph Waldo Emerson said "Common sense is genius dressed in its working clothes," he must have been talking about my dad. He taught me many worthwhile lessons, some merely by example. I didn't value these as a child, but looking back, I can see their significance.

One was his unusual way of solving problems. Seven children, all close in age, getting ready for school each morning was a circus. Most mornings, Dad delayed going to the office until the bus picked us up for school. One morning, though, he had an early appointment and was eating breakfast when we got up.

"Will someone find me a comb?" he asked.

Combs are regularly displaced when nine people are getting ready at the same time, especially with only one bathroom in the house. In our usual playful mood, we offered a fork, a toothbrush, a curry comb, a stiff clothes brush and a comb with only three teeth.

"Try this," one child suggested.

"Will this do?" another asked.

"See if this will work," I said.

We winked at each other and giggled, having great fun with our little game. Finally, my older sister brought him a comb, and he promptly rewarded her with a crisp, new five-dollar bill. In 1950, that was a lot of money. In 10 seconds flat, from every room in the house, we were able to recover 28 combs, all with the teeth intact. Of course, it was too late for another monetary handout. He had made his point.

His farm dealings were handled in much the same way; he solved each problem without upsetting anyone.

Once, he discovered that a lot of corn reserved for winter feeding was missing from the shed. He suspected one of the workers, but he didn't do anything about it for a while. When corn continued to disappear and he realized he might run short, he decided to act. He waited for the worker to start walking home through the field before he caught up with him on horseback. The young man was weighted down, carrying a sack of something bulky on his back.

"Charlie," Dad said, "that looks like a heavy load. What have you got there?"

"Oh, just some corn cobs I've been saving. I was taking them home for my wife to burn in the fireplace."

"Here, let me take those for you," Dad insisted, as he lifted the bag of corn onto the back of his horse.

When he got to the farmhouse, the wife met him on the porch. "Charlie's saved you some corn cobs to burn on the fire," Dad said, and he dropped the sack of corn on the porch. Dad could see through the problem to a logical solution; no more corn was ever missing.

Dad was a magistrate for a number of years, yet he never swore out a warrant. When people came to the house upset over a problem, he told them, "I've left the papers you need to fill out at the office. I'll bring them with me when I come home tomorrow." By the next day, they would usually cool off. "Second thoughts are sometimes the wisest," Dad would say.

On one occasion, a man who had been in a fistfight came into his office. "I want to swear out a warrant," he said. He was pacing back and forth, swearing with every step as he recalled the events leading up to the fight. Dad couldn't dissuade him in any way, so he gave the angry man the papers to fill out. When he finished answering all the questions, Dad said, "Now before I can serve this, there's one more thing you must sign."

"What's that?" he asked.

"You'll have to swear you're afraid of him."

"Afraid of him!" he screamed. "Why, I wouldn't swear to that if you gave me a million dollars," the man said, and he stormed out of the office, muttering under his breath all the way to his truck.

Dad's real love was horse trading. He was known throughout the country as a fair dealer. One sunny day, a fellow trader stopped by the farm. "Mr. Carter," he said to Dad, "I've got a horse that is identical in every way to one of yours. It has the same long mane and tail, the same brown and white markings, and is the same age. Why, they could pass for twins. So I was wondering what you'd take for yours."

Dad thought for a minute before answering. "I hadn't meant to sell, but if you're set on buying her, I'd take $300."

"Why, I couldn't give that much," the man said. "That's way too high."

"Well, then, I'll give you $300 for yours," Dad said.

They didn't trade that day; obviously, Dad's offer for the neighbor's horse wasn't enough. However, anyone can appreciate the common sense in Dad's offer.

Dad's been gone now for more than 40 years, but I am grateful for the lessons he taught me. I believe it was James Barrie who said "God gave us memory so that we might have roses in December."

Dorothy C. Rose

There Is So Much to Learn

One father is more than a hundred schoolmasters.

—George Herbert

Papa had a natural wisdom. He wasn't educated in the formal sense. When he was growing up at the turn of the century in a very small village in rural northern Italy, education was for the rich. Papa was the son of a dirt-poor farmer. He used to tell us that he never remembered a single day of his life when he wasn't working. The concept of doing nothing was never a part of his life. In fact, he couldn't fathom it. How could one do nothing?

He was taken from school when he was in the fifth grade, over the protestations of his teacher and the village priest, both of whom saw him as a young person with great potential for formal learning. Papa went to work in a factory in a nearby village, the very same village where, years later, he met Mama.

For Papa, the world became his school. He was interested in everything. He read all the books, magazines and newspapers he could lay his hands on. He loved to gather with people and listen to the town elders and learn about "the world beyond" this tiny insular region that was home to generations of Buscaglias before him. Papa's great respect for learning and his sense of wonder about the outside world were carried across the sea with him and later passed on to his family. He was determined that none of his

39

children would be denied an education if he could help it.

Papa believed that the greatest sin of which we were capable was to go to bed at night as ignorant as we had been when we had awakened that day. This credo was repeated so often that none of us could fail to be affected by it.

"There is so much to learn," he'd remind us. "Though we're born stupid, only the stupid remain that way."

To ensure that none of his children ever fell into the trap of complacency, he insisted that we learn at least one new thing each day. He felt that there could be no fact too insignificant, that each bit of learning made us more of a person and insured us against boredom and stagnation.

So Papa devised a ritual. Since dinner time was family time and everyone came to dinner unless they were dying of malaria, it seemed the perfect forum for sharing what new things we had learned that day. Of course, as children we thought this was perfectly crazy. There was no doubt, when we compared such paternal concerns with other children's fathers, Papa was weird.

It would never have occurred to us to deny Papa a request. So when my brother and sisters and I congregated in the bathroom to clean up for dinner, the inevitable question was, "What did you learn today?" If the answer was "Nothing," we didn't dare sit at the table without first finding a fact in our much-used encyclopedia. "The population of Nepal is . . . ," etc.

Now, thoroughly clean and armed with our fact for the day, we were ready for dinner. I can still see the table piled high with mountains of food. So large were the mounds of pasta that as a boy I was often unable to see my sister sitting across from me. (The pungent aromas were such that, over a half century later, even in memory they cause me to salivate.)

Dinner was a noisy time of clattering dishes and endless activity. It was also a time to review the activities of the day. Our animated conversations were always conducted in Piedmontese dialect since Mama didn't speak English. The events we recounted, no matter how insignificant, were never taken lightly. Mama and Papa always listened carefully and were ready with some comment, often profound and analytical, always right to the point.

"That was the smart thing to do."

"*Stupido*, how could you be so dumb?"

"*Cosi sia*, you deserved it."

"*E allora*, no one is perfect."

"*Testa dura* [Hardhead], you should have known better. Didn't we teach you anything?"

"Oh, that's nice."

One dialogue ended, and immediately another began. Silent moments were rare at our table.

Then came the grand finale to every meal, the moment we dreaded most—the time to share the day's new learning. The mental imprint of those sessions still runs before me like a familiar film clip, vital and vivid.

Papa, at the head of the table, would push his chair back slightly, a gesture that signified the end of the eating and suggested that there would be a new activity. He would pour a small glass of red wine, light up a thin, potent Italian cigar, inhale deeply, exhale, then take stock of his family.

For some reason this always had a slightly unsettling effect on us as we stared back at Papa, waiting for him to say something. Every so often he would explain why he did this. He told us that if he didn't take time to look at us, we would soon be grown and he would have missed us. So he'd stare at us, one after the other.

Finally, his attention would settle upon one of us. "Felice," he would say to me, "tell me what you learned today."

"I learned that the population of Nepal is . . ."

Silence.

It always amazed me, and reinforced my belief that Papa was a little crazy, that nothing I ever said was considered too trivial for him. First, he'd think about what was said as if the salvation of the world depended upon it.

"The population of Nepal. Hmmm. Well."

He would then look down the table at Mama, who would be ritualistically fixing her favorite fruit in a bit of leftover wine. "Mama, did you know that?"

Mama's responses were always astonishing and seemed to lighten the otherwise reverential atmosphere. "Nepal," she'd say.

"Nepal? Not only don't I know the population of Nepal, I don't know where in God's world it is!" Of course, this was only playing into Papa's hands.

"Felice," he'd say, "get the atlas so we can show Mama where Nepal is." And the search began. The whole family went on a search for Nepal.

This same experience was repeated until each family member had a turn. No dinner at our house ever ended without our having been enlightened by at least a half dozen such facts.

As children, we thought very little about these educational wonders and even less about how we were being enriched. We couldn't have cared less. We were too impatient to have dinner end so we could join our less-educated friends in a rip-roaring game of kick-the-can.

In retrospect, after years of studying how people learn, I realize what a dynamic educational technique Papa was offering us, reinforcing the value of continued learning. Without being aware of it, our family was growing together, sharing experiences and participating in one another's education. Papa was, without knowing it, giving us an education in the most real sense.

By looking at us, listening to us, hearing us, respecting our opinions, affirming our value, giving us a sense of dignity, he was unquestionably our most influential teacher.

I decided upon a career in teaching fairly early in my college years. During my training, I studied with some of the most renowned educators in the country. When I finally emerged from academia, having been generously endowed with theory and jargon and technique, I discovered to my great amusement that the professional educators were imparting what Papa had known all along. He knew there was no greater wonder than the human capacity to learn, that no particle of knowledge was too insignificant not to have the power to change us for the better.

"How long we live is limited," Papa said, "but how much we learn is not. What we learn is what we are. No one should miss out on an education."

Papa was a successful educator. His technique worked and has served me well all my life. Now, when I get home, often exhausted after a long working day's adventure, before my head hits the pillow I hear Papa's voice resound clearly in my room. "Felice," he asks, "what did you learn today?"

On some days I can't recall even one new thing I have learned. I'm surprised at how often this is the case (since most of us move in a world of the familiar and are too preoccupied to be bothered or challenged by the unfamiliar). I get myself out of bed and scan the bookshelves to find something new. Then, with that accomplished, Papa and I can rest soundly, assured that a day has not been wasted. After all, one never can tell when knowing the population of Nepal may prove to be a very useful bit of information.

Leo Buscaglia

One Last Lesson

As is a tale, so is life;
what matters is not how long it is,
but how good it is.

—Seneca

My father lay in his hospital bed, jaundiced and unconscious. His faint breathing signaled that he was still alive, just barely hanging on.

It was December 1982 and our family had just spent Christmas together—a reunion I had looked forward to since moving to Washington, D.C., for my first job that September. When Daddy met me at the airport gate with my mother, sister and brother-in-law, I could tell something was wrong. Always a robust man, he looked frail and old to me for the first time. He insisted on carrying my bags, but had to stop several times to catch his breath.

I asked him if something was wrong, but he just shrugged the question off and continued down the concourse.

Nick Belleris had never been one to complain. The first-born child of Greek immigrants, he was born on February 5, 1915, in Portland, Oregon. The family soon moved to Denver, where they settled down. As was the case with most immigrant families, the Bellerises struggled to make ends meet. Young Nick helped put food on the table by selling newspapers and shining shoes after school.

44

Tragedy struck my father young when both his parents died in 1937. Dad watched stoically as his younger brother and sister were sent to live with relatives in Iowa.

Dad fought in World War II, then came home and married my mother, Ruby, a young woman he'd known all his life. They soon started a family.

The GI Bill allowed Dad to go to business school. In partnership with two other men, he began Empire Meat Co., a wholesale meat packing house. My father rose each morning at 3:30 and spent his days hauling sides of beef in and out of a refrigerated room that reeked of raw meat and blood. It was a tough profession, but he did what he had to, to support his wife and two daughters. He never complained and never expected anything for himself.

He was happy just to come home, sit on the front porch on warm summer evenings and listen to baseball on the radio.

Now here he was, silently hanging on for his life. Just days earlier we had had a conversation about my job. I groused about my boss and how I sometimes dreaded going to work. With a far-off look in his eyes, Dad advised me, "Sometimes, you have to do things you don't want to do." It was a simple phrase I didn't fully understand at the time.

I soon grew to learn what my father was talking about. He had a relapse of prostate cancer that we thought had gone into remission in 1979. When the cancer returned in 1981, Dad decided to keep the news to himself.

He never told us why he kept this terrible secret, but I suspect it was to protect his family. He didn't want us to stop living because he was dying.

I was just finishing up college and moving on with my life by taking a job with a U.S. congressman. Had I known my father had only a few months to live, I never would have left, but he wouldn't spoil my opportunity and wished me luck.

Dad endured the pain that ravaged his body until I returned home for one last Christmas—to say good-bye in person. I watched helplessly as he took his last breath.

I look back now and realize what a strong, selfless act my

father committed. He taught me that sometimes you have to sacrifice for others, because that is what love is all about. Sometimes, you have to do things you don't want to do, and that makes all the difference.

Christine E. Belleris

My Father's Greatest Gift

*What greater ornament to a son
than a father's glory, or to a father than
a son's honorable conduct?*

—Sophocles

Christmas at West Point: I was an 18-year-old farm boy from Minnesota. Still a plebe, I couldn't leave the post even for Christmas. So for the first time, I expected to spend the holidays apart from my family.

Earlier that year I had almost given up and gone home. In Beast Barracks, we felt the pressure of the upperclassmen. This was 1949, and though some classmates had already earned commendations in World War II, even they were hazed. "Okay, hero," the upperclassmen would say, "tell us what you did to win that medal!"

When I told my folks I was thinking of returning home to attend the University of Minnesota, they said to do whatever I thought best. But then my older sister came on the phone: "Rand, everyone around here thinks you'll be coming back; it's too hard there." That was all I needed. I had no more thoughts of quitting.

Several weeks later, I got a letter from my dad. As he said, I was "all alone and far away," so he planned to come for a three-day visit. I was elated. When he arrived, I was cheered by his familiar lean face and firm handshake.

We walked past the snow-mantled parade grounds and glimpsed Christmas trees glimmering through the windows of the superintendent's and commandant's houses. We climbed the endless tier of stairs to the gothic Cadet Chapel to attend Christmas Eve services. I marveled once again at Dad's fine tenor voice as we sang the carols. Next day, under the large tree in the lobby of his hotel, we opened our presents. Then Dad had to get back to the rest of the family in Fergus Falls.

His brief visit was enough to revive and steel me for all that lay ahead.

Randolph V. Araskog gave me my first real instruction in life when, as a four-year-old, I went down to the barn each evening to watch him milk.

He had a gentle way with the cows and always said a soothing word to Sunset or Sunshine or Blackie. When all the milk was in the big dairy cans, I would get behind him and help push the two-wheeled cart up what was, for my short legs, an interminably long hill to the creamery.

Inside the creamery was the bottle washer. I would line up the bottles and Dad would expertly slide each onto the twirling brushes. That's where I first heard him sing his favorite song, "Old Refrain." It began: "I often think of home, dee-oo-lee-ay, when I am all alone and far away. . . ."

Dad had remarkable self-control and believed strongly in direct, clear communication. When I was 11, one day in the barn I climbed onto our new tractor. Not knowing it was in gear, I pulled the starter. The motor roared to life, the tractor jerked backward, and when those big knobby tires hit the barn wall, they started to climb. I killed the motor, and my frightened yells brought Dad running.

"Don't move," he said, his manner deliberate. Then, after chocking the front wheels so the tractor wouldn't lurch forward, he said, "All right, Rand. Hop down."

He hadn't raised his voice, but I was sure he was annoyed. He ended up asking a neighbor to help ease the tractor down. I felt terrible and pledged never to disappoint him again.

Five or six years later, however, I was out playing "ditch 'em" in Fergus Falls. That's a game where you try to outrun the other guy in your car. When I got home, Dad greeted me with the news that a police officer had dropped by. "Says you were going about 70. That right?" I admitted it was. "Don't do it again, Rand," he said. "I don't plan to talk to you about it further."

I later realized that the police officer knew he would get better compliance by saying a few words to my father than by giving me a ticket. This told me something about my father's reputation and made me even more intent on being worthy of his faith.

During my teens, the state began requiring expensive new pasteurization equipment, and Dad figured he would have to give up dairying. We moved into town, and he worked hard; but nothing came easy. He tried beekeeping, but came home covered with stings. He drove a bus for a local line, and then a school bus.

All this time, I was doing well in school, but I wasn't the only one studying. Evenings, Dad was cramming for a test, hoping to get work in the city assessor's office. Just about the time I was graduating first in my high-school class, he won a post as deputy city assessor.

One day our principal asked me if I wanted to go to West Point. It was a thrilling moment. Our Congressman, Harold C. Hagen, had heard of my record and wanted to sponsor my appointment.

After those difficult first months away from home, things began to look up—just as Dad, in his quiet way, suggested they would. "I've got a hunch," he liked to say, "that things will turn out for the best."

By the time I finished at West Point, Dad had succeeded to the position of city assessor. I was admitted to Harvard, where I studied Russian. Then, assigned to Army intelligence, I spent five years debriefing defectors, analyzing intercepts and acting as interpreter for high-ranking officials.

Returning home, I found Dad in his plainly furnished office in the city hall on the bank of the Otter Tail River. We propped our feet up, sipped coffee and talked of how tough it is to be true to yourself and yet deal fairly with people. He recalled how a member of our church, who didn't like the valuation he had put on her property, steamed into his office to protest. He heard her out, explained his valuation and stood his ground. Finally, she came around. "If you're right," he told me, "don't yield."

This advice served me well later on. In fact, my father's example in human relations has been more valuable to me than the advice of many experts. Some I paid as much as $200,000 a year for their counsel. My father's advice never cost me a cent, yet I found it more useful.

Throughout my years at ITT, I've tried to follow in his steps—to deal directly, to speak plainly, to keep faith with a plaque he once gave me: "All I have to give you is my good name. Pass it on."

In the winter of 1978-79, my parents took over our vacation home in New Jersey to escape the bitter Minnesota winter. My family and I went out from Manhattan each weekend to join them, and on Sunday mornings Dad and I would listen to a favorite radio program, *Music and the Spoken Word,* with the Mormon Tabernacle Choir.

There we sat, having coffee, listening to our program and then talking awhile before anyone else was up. Dad had some sense of the exciting days that were unfolding for me—already an executive vice-president of a large international conglomerate, but still a distance from the top. He knew, I think, that this was like the slope up to my own creamery, only now he was helping push *me* up that incline.

In the spring my folks returned to Minnesota, and so I listened to my favorite program alone. One week the music summoned memories of that Christmas at West Point. I called Dad and told him about the program—it wasn't broadcast in Fergus Falls—and how it had turned my thoughts back to 1949. "I hope you know your visit meant a lot to me," I said, and suggested we make it a point to talk each Sunday after the program. He was delighted.

Dad was 80 then, and every week, except when I was traveling, we talked. I would tell him about the music and the message, and then, with our coffee in hand, we'd reminisce. It gave each of us a strong start on the week ahead.

I think he was even more pleased than I when I finally was named chairman of ITT. And, in the following years, when I found myself immersed in difficult negotiations, I repeatedly turned to him for advice and counsel. "You're going to do fine, Rand," he would say. His delight in my success was all a son could ever hope for.

One Sunday morning, several years ago, an oh-so-familiar song closed the Mormon Tabernacle Choir program. I phoned my father and said, "Dad, just listen," holding the phone to the speaker. "The years have passed and gone, dee-oo-lee-ay, and though my heart is young, my head is gray. . . ."

Dad sighed and said how beautiful it was, and how fine it was of me to let him hear it. It struck me that both of our hearts were young, and yet, at 84, his hair was white and mine was beginning to gray.

Early one morning about two years later, the phone rang. I winced at my sister's voice, telling me as gently as she could that I couldn't call my father anymore.

A few weeks after his funeral, I sat once again in front of my radio and heard those beautiful words floating back from the choir, "When I am all alone and far away . . ."

For a moment I shuddered and truly felt alone. But then I thought of Christmas at West Point and the many Christmases since, and I realized how my father had enriched my life by his example and by a quiet authority that had nothing to do with wealth or power. The gift of a lifetime was set forth on that plaque: "All I have to give you is my good name. Pass it on."

Rand V. Araskog
chairman and CEO, ITT Corporation

He Retires

After 36 years
of standing rubber-booted
knee-deep in murky ponds
bent at the side of a Libyan river
seeing things most of us can't or refuse to see
after 36 years

of planning for fall and teaching and grading papers
but mostly
thinking
he retires

to think some more
to spend more time in the company of invertebrates
to savor a slug's trail
to marvel at a clam
to relish the world of a worm

he retires
his identity intact
his soul uncompromised

an uncommon man who never felt a need to
prove himself to anyone
a man who never once put on airs
a man who was unimpressed with his (or anybody else's) titles
a man whom his children can never recall saying a
mean thing about anybody
a man who chose to stay silent rather than tell a lie
a man who never had to act like a man because he was always
so much more

and despite the fact that his wife worried that
his thinking might get in her way
clutter up the life she had learned to live
he retires

to the pond
to his books
to his writings
to his thoughts
to his wife

who is glad she finally allowed him to retire

Jennifer Engemann

The Christmas
That Changed My Life

*Memory is more indelible
than ink.*

—Anita Loos

When I was a child growing up in Peekskill, New York, I used to dream of parachuting into the Soviet Union to find my father. Now, 40-some years later, a more earthbound version of my childhood fantasy was coming true. Looking through the bus window, I saw him standing on the sidewalk outside the Hotel Parnu in Parnu, Estonia, wearing a white cap and holding a bouquet of flowers. My heart beat wildly as I stepped off the bus.

I was born during World War II, on July 24, 1944, in Tartu, in Estonia, a small, beautiful country on the Baltic Sea, across from Finland. Both Hitler and Stalin took turns occupying Estonia, each trying to obliterate the national spirit. The Russians sent many Estonians, especially those who were educated or owned land, by cattle car to Siberia, or tortured them in town squares and left them to die as a warning to their neighbors.

In the late summer of 1944, my father, Egon Sildver, was stationed with an Estonian border-defense regiment trying to hold back the advancing Soviet Army as the Germans withdrew. Soviet soldiers were fighting right on our farm, and villagers rushed to the house, shouting to my mother, "You must go. You must go."

My mother took me and—along with her mother and both my father's parents—climbed into a wagon that was pulled by oxen. My mother took barely any belongings with her, just a few photographs.

She never saw my father or her home again. Traveling by wagons and later by cattle cars to the west, with little to eat, we joined thousands of other displaced persons escaping the battle. Along the way, my grandfather developed pneumonia and died. Meanwhile, my father returned to the farm and discovered that everyone in his life—his mother, his father, his wife, his baby—was gone! Imagine his desperation. He must have been frantic. Later, the Soviets arrested him, and he was imprisoned in Siberia until 1957. Exactly what had happened to him remained a mystery for many years because news from behind the Iron Curtain was so difficult to obtain.

My mother, my two grandmothers and I ended up in a refugee camp in Augsburg, West Germany, where we lived for five years, until 1950, when we were granted permission to immigrate to the United States. My mother had somehow learned that my father was a prisoner but that she could never be reunited with him because he was officially exiled for life. Eventually my father initiated a divorce.

An upbeat person, my mother worked in factories to support our family and often talked about her country, her family and the life she briefly shared with Egon Sildver, my father.

"He was so smart and so much fun—a wonderful person and a gentleman," my mother often told me. On her 21st birthday, she awoke to find her bedroom filled completely with freshly cut roses—his doing! She was 23 when I was born and passionately in love with him. She died 14 years ago at the age of 57.

Early in 1990, as the USSR was crumbling politically, I heard about an American travel agency arranging a group tour to Estonia in May. I was then working on Wall Street as an investment analyst, was happily married and the mother of two beautiful children—Eric is now 14, Kristin, 12—yet something was missing from my life. It was time to unravel the mystery of my father. My half sister Krista, a photographer, would go along.

Together Krista and I pored over old photographs my mother had treasured and searched through papers, pulling out anything official that might help trace my family's roots. I received little help or hope from the U.S. State Department or the Red Cross about the prospects of locating Egon Sildver. We were setting off with no definite plan and only this advice from the tourist agency: "Ask your guide when you arrive there."

Krista and I left for Tallinn, the capital of Estonia, on Thursday, May 24, 1990, armed with the old photos and documents. On the plane, studying the photos, I wondered if anyone would recognize this blue-eyed, 28-year-old man who must surely have changed since 1944. Could I find him? I didn't know what to think. I suspected the chances of his being alive were slim.

On May 25, we landed in an airport that seemed straight from a movie script—with dirty runways, rusty equipment, rickety trucks and grim-faced Soviet soldiers and officials everywhere. It was scary because the KGB, the Soviet secret police, was still very much in power. Almost everyone spoke Russian, the official language then, and I speak only the Estonian of a six-year-old, which sounds nothing like Russian.

Yet it wasn't all bleak. Later, out on the streets, the Estonians never stopped talking to us once they recognized us as Americans. The Soviets were quickly losing control over the Baltic countries of Estonia, Latvia and Lithuania, and as our multilingual tour guide, Vaike, had said to the entire group when she addressed us, "We are drunk with freedom. Please forgive us if we talk too much."

Not long after being greeted by Vaike, I asked her for help in my search. "Later," she replied, brushing me aside. She acted busy, uninterested and perhaps a little suspicious. The next morning, however, when Krista and I were the only people to show up for her scheduled tour, she softened. "Let me call my relatives in Tartu," she said. "Perhaps they can help."

Help, in fact, soon came from every direction. From the women in babushkas we met in the washroom of a theater, to an anesthesiologist named Liia whom we befriended at dinner and who then took Tuesday off from work to join us tramping into and out of government registries, everyone volunteered support. It was deeply gratifying. Liia made telephone calls. "I have an American friend, and she is looking for her father," she explained to a brother-in-law, Priit, in Tartu. The search for my father began to build steam in ways even unbeknownst to us as Krista and I trooped from bureau to bureau bribing unsmiling officials with American cigarettes and lipsticks.

We'd been in Estonia less than a week. On Wednesday in Tartu, where we'd gone for a day's search, a woman in a registry eyed the photo of my father and made a startling announcement: "I know this man. He used to be my neighbor here in Tartu, but he moved to Parnu in 1962."

A lead—we finally had a lead!

Parnu was hours away, on the Baltic Sea, and our government-approved trip didn't include an excursion there. It wasn't easy working with the Soviet officials, but by Thursday evening a bus trip and a day of searching in Parnu had been set up for Friday. Vaike would bring her daughter, Inge, along to help with the work of translation.

Thursday about 6 P.M. the telephone rang at our hotel in Tallinn. I was exhausted emotionally and physically when I picked up the receiver. There was a man's voice on the line, and even though he spoke Estonian, I could understand him perfectly. I slipped easily into my early tongue.

"*Terre, kas see on Liina Sildver?*" he said. [Is Liina Sildver there?]

"Yes, this is Liina Sildver," I replied in Estonian.

"Yah. This is your father," he answered. As simple as that.

I was flooded with emotion. He was so calm, so supportive, so loving from the moment we began to speak. Immediately I could see that everything my mother had said about Egon Sildver was true.

"My darling Liina," he said.

"We are coming to Parnu," I said. "By bus. Tomorrow." I went on: Where would he be? How would I recognize him?

"I will meet you," he said. "I will be waiting for you in front of the Hotel Parnu, and I will be wearing a white hat."

Everyone on the bus knew my story and was keyed up. People

were starting to cry, Vaike told me later. I was oblivious to others as I got off the bus to meet my father after all these years.

"My dear, good, unforgettable daughter," he said. But his hug is what I will never forget. Both arms embraced me. He was holding flowers. They were for me. I was crying. He was crying. The last time my father held me I was six weeks old.

He and I would just look at each other and our eyes would well up on that first day.

"People have been coming to my home," he said. Because he had no telephone—he'd been on a waiting list for 20 years! Strangers had been knocking on his door with the news of our arrival.

"'Your American daughters are looking for you,' they said. This is a very rare miracle. I will remember forever. You, too, must feel it can't be explained," he told me that beautiful day. Even the weather was perfect. We walked together. He took charge right away and got us a taxi to go to his home. Lilacs were blooming. Their scent was intense. My father bought little bouquets of lilies of the valley from a street vendor for all the women, including Vaike, whose hand he kissed as he bent on one knee with a deep bow of gratitude. At the front door of his home, a three-room apartment in a gray, square building, he said, "Open the door. Go in first. This is your home, too."

I felt sad—sad for the years we had lost—but happy, amazed and grateful that I'd found him.

We met his wife, Liidia, whom he married while a prisoner in Siberia. As he tried to explain to me, Liidia gave him a reason to live and, in fact, brought him back from death when he weighed only 80 pounds. She and my half sister Tiina welcomed us warmly, with food and champagne my father had saved for a special occasion. Then he and I talked, walked, cried and spent the rest of that afternoon together.

Since that initial reunion crammed with hugs, walks along the Baltic Sea, tears, shared stories and promises, my father and I have been making up for lost time. We pledged then to know each other well, and he writes letters by the bundles, which arrive two and sometimes three times a week at my home in Glen Ridge, New Jersey.

His first trip to the United States to see me was a Christmas visit. I had tried to push him toward traveling during a warmer, less stressful time of year, but he was adamant. After months of wrangling with the Soviet bureaucracy, he finally got his visa approved. Christmas was wonderful. His gift to me, an Estonian wool folk skirt, had been handmade by his wife. Our presents for him—piles of American gadgets, a bathrobe, custom-tailored dress slacks—amazed him. "Too much, too much," he said often. Fascinated by the paper as he opened gifts, he planned to take it all back to Estonia, where colorful gift-wrap was unheard of. The fresh fruit in our amazing American supermarkets stunned him, too.

My family feels more complete now. That Christmas seemed to bring us together like a colorful jigsaw puzzle, with all its pieces finally assembled. My husband, Peter, enjoys my father immensely. Eric and Kristin, who lost a grandfather when Peter's dad died recently, now have their "new" grandfather securely fixed in their minds. And anxious for his own story to have meaning for them, he has written a long, detailed account of what happened to him, addressed "To my children and grandchildren."

Perhaps the highlight of his weeks spent with us was his beautiful toast at Christmas dinner. A very emotional man who loves to talk, he rose from the table, clinked his glass to get everyone's attention and, using his English, explained that in Roman times if someone got up and was a "long talker," the people would make him stand on one leg so he wouldn't be able to talk long.

"This is a one-legged toast," he said, laughing. "For weeks you have all asked me what I think of America and how I feel being here with you. I want you to know that I feel as if I have been hypnotized and this is all a dream. . . . Have you ever heard a beautiful piece of music? That's how I feel. Have you ever read a beautiful poem? That's how I feel. There aren't words to describe my feelings."

I'm still overwhelmed by this wonderful man. He's become real to me, of course, and I have twinges of guilt when I can't manage to write three letters a week in answer to his. Yet I see things as he does, and the familiarity is so comfortable, even in our hybrid letters, part English and part Estonian. Words, in fact, can't possibly describe this connection we share.

Liina Sildver Broms
as told to Maryann B. Brinley

Letters from My Father

The simplest and shortest ethical precept is to be served by others as little as possible, and to serve others as much as possible.

—Leo Tolstoy

I often wonder whether anyone can beat my father's record of letter writing. While I was doing graduate work in Edinburgh and London, he wrote to me every other day for three years. He was a good writer. Writing came easily to him, but still, writing every other day for three years was remarkable.

In spite of his busy schedule, he maintained this record because he knew I was desperately homesick for my family in Hong Kong. And I wrote back. It did not matter if it was three in the morning, I would write. Before the first collection of mail, I would run across the huge grounds in the middle of the four residential halls to drop off my letter. Then I waited for the end of the day when I returned from lectures to find the letters that sustained, encouraged and comforted me. He always addressed me as "My most beloved daughter, Shuet."

My father was a gentle man. He was also a gentleman, an accomplished man. He did not earn a doctoral degree but in those days, how many did? He was exceptionally good at Chinese literature and often put my brother and me to shame when he could memorize

61

pages of poetry that we had learned but promptly forgotten. He was very knowledgeable about Chinese history and familiar with Western literature. When he studied English literature, his thesis was on Oscar Wilde, but somehow he managed to persuade his professor to allow him to write his thesis in Chinese! A self-made man, he was the first in his family to have a college education, and he taught for many years. It is said that he was such a popular teacher, he could make even a piece of chalk sound interesting.

Like many other Chinese families that fled China when the Communists took over in the late 1940s, we lost all that we had. Although my mother came from a wealthy family, she lost most of her possessions during the war. We were poor. My father would teach during the day and write movie scripts at night. He must have had quite a reputation because movie producers would pay for him to stay at a modest hotel for a few nights while he worked feverishly to finish a script.

I could imagine how tired he was, working day and night. He slept little. But he never complained. We lived in a school building in Wanchai where we were given a tiny ten-by-six-foot room. My parents slept in that room. The rest of us waited until the night classes were finished, then we would lay our mats on the floor in the classroom. Those were our beds.

We had little; we asked for no more. We knew our parents did the best they could and dared not ask for more. I remember vividly how we invented games when I was seven or eight years old and my brother was three or four. We would hide under a table and pretend we were in a house. My brother collected hundreds of soda-bottle caps. Those were his soldiers. He could play for hours, fighting his imaginary battles. On occasion, we were fortunate enough to receive free tickets for the movies from friends in the entertainment business. For our birthdays, we ate at the Americana, an inexpensive restaurant where we would devour two or three spring chickens. I have had many delicious dinners since then at posh restaurants, but those spring chickens are the best I've ever had. I never really felt deprived.

Just when life seemed to be unfolding smoothly, when my parents' hard work had gradually lifted us out of poverty, and when my brother and I were succeeding with our education and careers, we were shaken by the news that our father—who was the image of good health—was diagnosed with pancreatic cancer. I flew to Hong Kong to be with my father. His cancer was inoperable, and the doctors gave him a year to live. That May, I should have had three birthdays: the Western birthday and two lunar birthdays (my lunar birthday fell on a leap month). But we did not celebrate any of my birthdays in 1981.

On May 1, 1982, my husband and I flew from our home in San Francisco to Hawaii. We were greeted at the airport by my good friend Rosanna. When I saw her, I immediately knew why she was there. We flew home to Hong Kong immediately, but I have never forgiven myself for not being there with my father in his final hours.

The funeral was a spectacular event. To this day, I still cannot fully appreciate what the funeral service means in Western society. A celebration of the life of the deceased? A closure? In Hong Kong, the funeral is very significant and represents a person's success in every endeavor, but especially on the human-relationship level. For my father's funeral, flower arrangements sent by mourners overflowed into the streets. People of all ages and from all sectors of Hong Kong society came to pay their respects.

Father was one of those rare people who had few enemies and scores of admirers. He was paid the highest compliment when a friend commented, "This funeral dwarfs even the funeral of the shipping magnate, H. Y. Tung."

One year after my father passed away, my daughter, Laura, was born. Four years later my son, Paul, was born. I believe wholeheartedly that my father was watching over me when my children came into this world. Between the loving care of both God and my father, I was in good hands. I am by nature reticent when it comes to talking about myself, but I want to tell my children about the grandfather they never had the privilege and pleasure of knowing. Perhaps one day, they will even learn to read the many letters written in Chinese that I have kept—sent to me by my beloved father.

Mo-Shuet Tam

A Letter to My Son

Just as children learn from Dad's example, Dad himself can learn from the experiences of fatherhood. Parents *magazine invited fathers to share a moment from their lives that gave special meaning to fatherhood. The following two letters from father to son were responses to that invitation.*

Dear Jay:

When you were about five months old, my routine was, after a long day at work, to pick you up from day care. When we got home, I'd set you down while I changed; we'd play for a bit (usually a game of Amazing Flying Diaper, which made you kick and giggle as I swooped the diaper past your face). Then I'd change and feed you. On most nights, a nap would follow. Mommy would be home about an hour later.

The routine was short and sweet, but workmanlike. I found myself rushing through that precious hour and a half we had alone. I had come from a large family and was thrilled with the idea of starting my own. But once the honeymoon of your infant days was over, it seemed that all I wanted to do was put you through your paces and get you off to bed or into your mother's arms so I could read, write or listen to music. Time was short, and I was feeling squeezed.

One night I tried something different. When we came home, I stripped to my underwear, changed you, set you on my bed and jumped on with wild abandon! We tumbled, hugged, snuggled.

64

I lifted and twirled you again and again, until you were laughing about as hard as anyone I'd ever heard. I hoped that you wouldn't mind if dinner ran a little late so we could keep at it.

We were both still laughing when we finally lay down on the bed, facing each other, my arm around you. Suddenly we stopped as we caught each other's glance. It lasted maybe half a minute, but it seemed much longer. Inches apart, our eyes were glued. Had we ever really looked at each other? Not like this. Smiling, your eyes bright and full of glee, you realized who I was for the first time. It was a perfect moment.

When Mommy came home that night, I felt as if I was holding the world's biggest secret.

"You know what happened tonight," I said. "Jay told me he loved me."

"Really!" she said. "I didn't know that five-month-olds could talk."

Oh, but you did, Jay. I heard you loud and clear.

Love,
Dad

Rob Kinslow

Dear Jack:

When you were born, I was in a faraway place flying airplanes for the navy. Deployment was important to me, but still I felt guilty not being there for your birth. Mom and I endured the separation, and for a month we counted the days until I would meet you.

On the airplane, as we were finally heading home, it felt as if the entire squadron was as excited as I was. Naturally I was the first person off the plane, running to your beautiful mom and this tiny little bundle zipped up in a blue snowsuit—my son. I couldn't say anything. I was too choked up. I didn't want to let go of you, even to load my luggage into the car. If only you could understand what I felt that first moment, you holding my finger, asleep in my arms.

Mom and I got home, tired and exhausted from such an emotional roller coaster. I wasn't too tired, however, to notice that you had your mom's nose and my eyes (not to mention my hairline). Mom and I talked and dreamed about the fun we would have with you and what we thought you would be when you grew up. I had no doubt that you and I were going to be best buddies. As the evening wore on, Mom and I were drained, but you were still awake. So I decided to stay up with you, while your mom went to bed.

After getting my first chance to change your diaper, I brought you back downstairs. I turned on the television, and as luck would have it, the San Francisco 49ers were playing on Monday night football. I turned out all the lights, lay down on the couch and put you on my chest. I was so afraid that my big hands were going to drop you, but I held on. It wasn't five minutes later that you fell asleep, once again holding my finger. I didn't move for the entire game because I didn't want to wake you. Jack, it was at that moment I realized that I was a Dad and that you, your mom and I were a family.

I know you won't remember any of this, but that day meant everything to me. And no matter how many times I tell this story to my friends, it always puts a smile on my face. I am so proud and excited to be your dad!

Love,
Dad

John Barnet

Reprinted from the August 1992 issue of *Parents* magazine.

Daddy's Words

True wit is nature to advantage dress'd,
What oft was thought, but ne'er so well express'd.

—Alexander Pope

Daddy loved words. *Badinage* and *persiflage* were among his favorites, both as words and in actual usage as spice for his conversations. He would have been completely at ease bantering away the evening with the legendary wits of Alice Toklas's time. Unfortunately, he got stuck with me.

I had asthma. Some nights I could hardly breathe and I couldn't sleep, so Daddy would hold me on his lap in his big rocking chair. I was only five, but I vividly remember those nights—not only how they made me feel better, but the things my father taught me.

"What kind of a noise annoys an oyster?" he'd ask. "A noisy noise annoys an oyster."

"Moses supposes his toes-es are roses, but Moses supposes erroneously; for Moses, he knows-es his toes-es aren't roses, as Moses supposes his toes-es to be."

Daddy knew dozens of speech exercises and dozens of stories and poems with Aesopic morals. I became fairly adept at repeating them with him until I could breathe easier and felt sleepy. Then he'd carry me up to bed and tuck me in.

It was years later that I learned why Daddy had so emphasized "round, pear-shaped tones" as I repeated his little ditties and homilies. My father had attended what was then called Emerson School of Elocution in Boston. Through his aptitude for languages, he passed down to me a great appreciation for English, French and Latin.

As I grew older and outgrew the asthma attacks, I found that my interest in Daddy's propensity toward the use of longer, more unusual words grew stronger.

Mother was a cute, diminutive person who ruled her household with strictness and love. With six children and a husband to care for, she found little time for tutoring us in vocabulary. If Mother would say we children were often guilty of "putting off" doing our chores, Daddy would say we "procrastinated." When Mother said, "There's a lot of lightning in this storm," Daddy said, "Look at this pyrotechnical display!"

When I attended high school and college, what really impressed me was not only his love for grammar, syntax and pronunciation, but also the way in which he could make words work for him. I recall one particular instance when he was asked to write a letter of recommendation for one of my sister's schoolmates who was applying for admission to nursing school.

Daddy was acting chief of police in our small town at that time and was well acquainted with practically everyone in town. He certainly knew Marie and her family.

Marie's father was an alcoholic, and it was well known that her mother accompanied Marie's father to the local tavern on many occasions. Daddy was also aware that Marie had been caught shoplifting at two of the local stores. Still, he thought Marie should have a chance to prove herself. He must have figured she probably would, if given a chance to get away from her home environment. So he wrote as glowing a recommendation as he could. I remember that it ended, "Marie has taking ways." Daddy explained, "In case anyone ever asks me why I didn't tell about her shoplifting, I can truthfully say I revealed it in the last sentence of my letter."

During the summer after my first year in college, Daddy received a letter from his brother Tom's son. Wally had just finished an exhaustive study of their family genealogy. He was pleased and excited to report that he had traced it back with certainty to Charlemagne. *"Au droit ou à sinestre?"* Daddy asked wryly, as he finished reading Wally's letter aloud. "I've read that Charlemagne sired some 27 illegitimate children."

In either case, my older sister Lucy and I were thrilled to find out about Daddy's familial connections. We already had records of Mother's family tree, back on her mother's side through King Godin of Norway, and on her father's side through Queen Ena of Spain. We told Daddy that it meant a great deal to us to know his side of the tree, too.

"Yes," Daddy said. "You children are entitled to a coat of arms depicting peerage, nobility and royalty. That's feathers, ermine and a lion, you know. And I trust you will bear this in mind in later years. Mark my words, knowing your genealogy should prove of immeasurable assistance to you while you're washing your dishes!"

I've often wondered why he didn't use some fancy term for dish washing. I think it must be because there is none, or Daddy would have known it.

Barbara B. Griffin

My Father, the Biker

*Nothing in life is to be feared;
it is only to be understood.*

—Marie Curie

My father, a bank vice-president in Little Rock, Arkansas, was in Dallas for two weeks at a conference, so I decided to tell him about my motorcycle.

Recently out of graduate school, I had a real job and a steady income for the first time. The rent for my apartment was cheap, and because I had lived for years on student loans, so were my tastes; saving money was a snap. After a few months I splurged and wrote the biggest check of my life to buy the one thing—maybe the only thing—my parents would never have bought for me: a motorcycle.

Late at night, returning along spooky, deserted freeways from a party or visiting friends, I would accelerate to 90 or 100 MPH on the straightaways, my torso low over the gas tank. I rocked in and out of curves, pleased and amazed, like a child with a gyroscope, by the conjunction of balance and speed.

I met my father at his hotel room and said, "Come on down to the parking lot. I want to show you something." He followed me to the parking space where my black 1981 Honda CX500 was leaning nonchalantly on its kickstand. My father put his hands on his hips, looked at the bike and then at me.

"Give me the key," he said, and for a moment, although I was 25 years old and financially independent of him, I felt like a teenager again, being grounded. I dug into my jeans pocket and produced the key.

My father put it in the ignition and slung his right leg over the saddle. He looked down at the foot pegs and gearshift, gripped and released the clutch with his left hand and the brake with his right. "One down, four up?" he asked.

"Yeah," I said, surprised he knew anything about the gearing pattern of a motorcycle.

"Is there a helmet law in Texas?" he asked.

"No."

He pressed the starter and the engine turned over crisply. He clicked the gear into neutral with the toe of his black, wing-tipped shoe and back-stepped the bike out of the parking place.

"Uh, where are you going?" I asked.

"Just around the block," he said, and throttled up, lurching a little as he rolled out of the parking lot and onto the street. He went around the corner and out of sight.

The image of his business shirt rippling across his back remained in my mind for a moment. Of the many reactions I had anticipated from him, hopping on my bike and riding off was not even in the ballpark. After what seemed an eternity, my father appeared around the corner and pulled smoothly into the parking place.

He then told me about a motorcycle he had owned when he was 18. "When I was in the service at the Jacksonville air base, I had an old Harley-Davidson Flathead 74, not the kind with the overhead valves," he said. "It had a shift on the side. I was cruising along on the old Jacksonville highway, going about 45 or 50 miles an hour, when I saw a block of wood on the road. I had on hard-toe military safety shoes and decided to see what would happen if I kicked that block of wood." He started to smile. "I thought I would never get the feeling back in my leg. It was numb for about 30 minutes." He laughed. "Don't ever do anything like that."

Toward the end of that summer, a friend and I rode our bikes to Hot Springs, Arkansas, to visit my parents at their vacation condo. I knew that my mother now was going to find out about my purchase. As we rode up to their apartment complex, she happened to be standing on the balcony. I took my helmet off, expecting her to be upset, but she showed no emotion. After my friend left and my mother and I were alone, I asked her what she thought of the motorcycle.

"You're old enough to do what you want," she said. "Does your father know about this?"

I nodded.

"Did he ride it?" This was a question I hadn't expected.

"Yes, he did."

"Did you lose sight of him?" she asked. Another unexpected question.

"Yes."

"Were you nervous?"

I thought back. "Yeah, a little."

"See, now you know how I feel," she said.

I moved to New York a few years later, and my cousin agreed to keep the bike for me in Arkansas. During visits back there, I still ride it occasionally, but now I think of my mother and her comment. I don't want to make her nervous. The bike has become mere transportation.

My father goes over and starts it up every now and then, just to make sure it still runs.

Jay Jennings

A Leather-Necked Farmer

There is no season such delight can bring,
As summer, autumn, winter, and the spring.

—William Browne

Tears well in my eyes when I think of my daddy, his rough neck and those early years growing up on the farm, Barefoot-n-Cotton. Those were the carefree days, when life was simple compared with life today, half a century later. Those years were filled with memories and feelings deeply rooted within my being.

Today, misty-eyed, I visualize an older man braving the elements of nature. His weathered neck, filled with deep crevices and creases, became the symbol of long, hard hours spent in the cotton fields at home. Thoughts of Daddy remind me of the smell of earth after a downpour, the surprise of a ladybug alighting on my hand, the itch to go barefoot, and the longing to be a childlike spirit, free and innocent. In my mind, these images recall an era of simplicity— of wide-open spaces under clear skies and crisp, pure air.

My father was a proud man of humble means who worked long, strenuous hours, from sunup to sundown, and occasionally into the wee hours of night. Through days of toil, he made his farm into a prosperous operation that my brothers, William, Harold and Allen, continue to cultivate today. When I was a youngster, this leather-necked farmer was my ideal, my hero, my strength, my protector and my greatest teacher.

Following him throughout my formative years, I was richly blessed by sampling God's handiwork first-hand, on a daily basis, in the garden of life. Through his gentle guidance, I learned patience, appreciation for the simple things, the importance of hard work in making a living, how to organize my life, how to prepare before beginning a project and how to meet challenges face-to-face.

I also learned the basics of life: honesty, trust, self-respect, motivation and responsibility for my own actions. My father was a professor at a rural university under the skies. A capable man, not without flaws, he was as much a part of the land our forefathers had left him as the stalks of cotton that flourished in the valley.

Through the chill of winter and the blistering summer sun, this man tilled the land. Daily, the elements of nature beat upon his neck, planting rows and rows of lines and deep crevices, marking his labor. His golden years' trademark, a weathered neck, became a symbol of all he stood for and all he had imparted to me, and a bittersweet reminder of my past, when life was simple.

Patsy P. Lewis

The Pheasant

*I cannot think of any need in childhood as strong
as the need for a father's protection.*

—Sigmund Freud

Growing up on a farm provided a daily opportunity to see how mankind and nature are interrelated. Both of my parents had a supreme sense of respect for Mother Nature and everything in her realm. This was demonstrated time and time again in my childhood, and was personified by the events of one particularly memorable day in early spring.

The bright sun filtered through the clouds, warming the fields of alfalfa that my father was mowing. Within a day or two it would be put into bales of hay, gathered from the field, stored in the hay loft and used to feed our livestock. I stood at the fence line with the lunch my mother had prepared for my father, watching as he cautiously guided the tractor up and down the field, head down, eyes closely observing the movements of the mower. As he neared the end of the field, Dad saw me holding out the lunch for him. He stopped and motioned that it was safe for me to bring it to him.

"Please, Daddy, take me for a ride," I begged as he ate his lunch. I loved riding on the tractor with my father. It was quite a treat because children were forbidden from riding it alone; it was for grown-ups only. Extremely safety-conscious, Dad rarely allowed us children to even be near it, let alone climb up on this big "dangerous" machine. So protective was he of his family, he seldom asked my mother to drive the tractor even short distances—such as to fuel it—around the farmstead.

I also liked riding on the tractor because I relished the feel of the wind blowing through my hair and the warm sun on my face, arms and legs. But most of all, I loved being close to my father; sitting near him on the tractor seat inside his protective arms was a very loving feeling, and I adored my daddy and everything about him. I found his high energy and love for the outdoors contagious; his charisma exciting; and his running commentary about everything around him interesting—nothing escaped his eyes: birds, bees, flowers, clouds, passing cars and trucks. All became fodder for a comment, story or lesson.

"Please, Daddy, can't I ride with you?" I asked again.

"No, no. It's not safe for you to be on the open tractor; I never know when the long sharp sickle of the mower will come dangerously close to a nesting pheasant or a rabbit or a fox. When that happens, I have to stop suddenly, and that could cause you to fall. No, I'll give you a ride another time."

"Oh, please, Daddy. I'll be so careful. I'll stay out of your way. Take me with you for a little ways, and then I'll get off and I won't complain even if it's a long way home."

It never took too much begging with my father. When his children wanted to be with him, he was a soft touch.

I sat on the edge of the tractor seat between my father's legs, holding on to his knees, trying as hard as I could not to get in his way as he constantly shifted from side to side. With the skill of a surgeon, Dad began by first looking ahead as he aligned the tractor with the meticulously straight line of still-standing alfalfa—a sharp contrast to the stems, cut off from their life source by the mower, now lying flat against the ground. After he did this he shifted to look behind, continuously observing the long row of the razor-sharp sickle blade as it deftly sliced millions of hearty alfalfa stalks the instant it came into contact with them. One powerful arm steered the tractor while the other arm wrapped around his 10-year-old daughter, protecting her in its grip.

Suddenly a pheasant squawked and jerked skyward, and in the same instant my father instinctively stepped on the clutch. As the tractor lurched to a halt, my father flung both his arms around me, stopping me from being thrown into the steering wheel or off the tractor.

Protecting me had made it impossible to save the female pheasant minding her nest. As quickly and sharply as she rose into the sky, she fell from it, hitting the ground with a deadening thump, then violently and aimlessly thrashing around. Both her legs had been severed near her body.

"Oh, no," my father said softly, getting down from the tractor and lifting me off with him. He hurried over to the wounded bird, picked her up and, with tears in his eyes, stroked her beautiful sleek feathers, apologizing to her for the pain he had caused.

He shook his head and said in a voice that housed as much disgust as it did passion, "She can never live this way." He was talking as much to the universe as he was to me. "She'll be easy prey to any predator," he added, and in his next breath, he took hers. With one quick flick of my father's wrist, she no longer had to contemplate her fate in the wild.

He flung the head of the now-decapitated bird far away from us. Then gently pulling the bird's wings together, he held her upside down so that her blood would drain from her body and not be absorbed into the meat, which would have made it inedible.

Over the years I had often experienced the killing of fowl: chickens, turkeys, geese and ducks all made their way to our table in a similar fashion. I was saddened as much by my father's sense of devastation as from having witnessed the bird's death.

Dad gathered up the three orphaned eggs from the pheasant's nest, which now lay in disarray, and placed them in the empty lunch box that sat alongside the pheasant, and home we went.

My mother prepared the pheasant for dinner that evening. At the supper table, my father talked about the nature of Mother Nature, and our role in protecting and comforting all her creatures. His sadness had been replaced by his appreciation for such an excellent dinner and the safety of family at his side.

We children were taken by surprise. We had come to the table fully prepared to mourn alongside our father. I had shared with all my brothers and sisters the sequence of events and Dad's reaction: we felt sad for him as well as the pheasant. But our father wasn't sad at all; in fact, he seemed jubilant. We children didn't understand his changed mood. After all, we were all still a bit sad—and not at all sure if we were going to take a helping of the roast pheasant now nestled in the glass baking dish.

"Daddy, why didn't we let the pheasant live?" my sister Judy inquired. "She could still sit on her eggs and hatch them, even without legs."

"Without legs," Dad answered, "the mother pheasant would no longer be able to teach her chicks to hunt after they hatched. And worse, without legs, she couldn't protect herself against predators like the fox. No, I'm afraid she wouldn't make it out there without legs."

Always the humanitarian, my brother Mark chided, "Daddy, no one, not even a hungry old fox, would hurt a poor pheasant who didn't have legs."

"Legs or no legs," responded my father, "a fox will eat a pheasant any day, any time of day."

"That's not very nice," cried my littlest brother.

"Why?" I questioned. "Why would a fox want a wounded bird?"

"Because," replied my father, "it's in his nature."

We all looked curious and confounded. Sensing that he had not been completely understood, our father leaned forward, rested both elbows on the table and, with his best storytelling voice and most animated face, began his yarn. "Once upon a time, there was a pheasant who, while out foraging for food, broke both her wings. And since her wings were broken, she couldn't fly. Now this was a real big problem because her home was on the other side of the lake, and she wanted to get there. She stood by the edge of the lake thinking what to do. She flapped and flapped her wings, but it was no use; she was too injured to fly.

"Along came a fox who, seeing the pheasant's problem, said, 'Looks like you have a problem. What's the matter?'

"'Oh,' said the pheasant, 'I live on the other side of the lake, and I've broken my wings, and now I can't fly home.'

" 'What a coincidence!' said the fox. 'I live on the other side of the lake, too, and I'm on my way home. Why don't you hop on my back, and I'll give you a ride.'

" 'But you're a fox, and you will eat me,' said the pheasant.

" 'No, no,' said the fox. 'Don't be afraid. Hop on. I'll take you home.'

"So the pheasant, anxious to get home, hopped on the fox's back, and he began the swim home. But just before they reached the shore on the other side of the lake, the fox shook the pheasant from his back, causing her to fall into the water. Frightened, the pheasant cried out, 'Oh, please don't eat me.'

" 'I'm afraid I have to,' said the fox.

" 'But why?' pleaded the pheasant.

" 'Because,' grinned the fox, 'it's in my nature.'"

With differing degrees of understanding—and deep in thought—we children quietly began eating, absorbing the visions of the story we had just heard. And so it was that the taste of pheasant was made delicious to me—and became symbolic of the nature of Mother Nature and of my father's understanding of it and respect for it.

The pheasant's three eggs were given to a plump old goose who dutifully sat on the eggs around the clock, getting up from the nest only briefly to eat and to turn the eggs. Within weeks, three pheasant chicks emerged. After several weeks of caretaking, we released them into the wild, making the cycle complete: my father had taken from Mother Nature and given back to her as well. In making the exchange, he taught us a bit more about the nature of Mother Nature and our role in protecting and comforting those in it. And to hold her in the highest regard—as much as we did our father.

Bettie B. Youngs

My Father's Voice

*Blessed indeed is the man who hears
many gentle voices call him father!*

—Lydia M. Child

It has been almost 30 years since I last heard my father's voice, but the echoes remain. I can still hear the slightly flat Midwestern accent, strangely rough and soft at the same time. I can still hear him singing loud and off key, whistling as he worked in his garden, whispering to my mother, calling out to my sisters and me.

I am the youngest of my father's seven children. He was in his late 40s, soon to be a grandfather, when I was born; I was only 10 when he died. He taught me many lessons in those few years we shared, but they were the lessons of childhood.

He taught me that if we sat very, very quietly and very, very patiently in a corner of the front yard, the squirrels would come to us. He taught me to sing "Red River Valley" and that watching westerns on television was a fine way to spend a Saturday evening. He tried to teach me that vanilla ice cream was better than chocolate. He succeeded in teaching me to always honor my mother and never to lie to my parents.

When it was time for the lessons of adolescence and adulthood, he was gone. Yet his influence on all of his children remained and has grown through the years, multiplied by the influence we have on each other. We do not all remember him the same way. We have different memories, different visions and different lives. I still live in my father's house. It is mine and my husband's now, but my father's presence is here. Photographs of him hang on the walls, an enduring reminder as the memories fade. I recently talked with all my brothers and sisters, wanting and needing to know what they each remembered.

"What is the most important lesson you learned from Daddy?" I asked each of them.

"Faith," says the sister whose belief in herself may sometimes waver but whose trust in God remains constant. Her overflowing warmth comforts us all.

"Fidelity to principle," says the brother who has stood alone in turmoil strong enough to shake the surest foundation. He has never lost his temper, never been less than a total gentleman.

"He showed me that great calmness and great strength often go together," says the brother who opposed our father and confronted him head-on. They both stood their ground and held fast to their principles. Through the conflict, they grew to love and respect each other more.

"Hard work," says the brother who toils in the sun and on the water. He works long hours without complaining, knowing that the hardest work brings the greatest satisfaction.

"Morals," says the sister who remains my lifelong model on how to be a good daughter, a good wife and, especially, a good mother.

"Family first, always," says the sister who works full-time, attends college part-time and has never missed seeing her sons play in a baseball game. When my daughter was an infant, this sister came over to my house daily, on her coffee break, to cuddle her newborn niece.

These are all lessons from my father, filtered through my brothers and sisters and the way they have lived their lives.

I think of my father when I walk out onto the patio he built, behind the house he built—where he raised his children and where I am now raising mine.

As I stand and look over the tops of the white-budded camellias he planted, now grown as tall as trees, and see the same pines he saw so many years ago still swaying in the wind, I know the most important lesson I learned from my father: that home is the heaven you make for yourself on earth. It is where you can smell the flowers and feel the breeze and where, if you are very, very quiet, you can sense your father's presence all around you.

And now, 30 years later, when we are all together—brothers and sisters, husbands, wives, sons and daughters—our voices and our laughter come together and form one voice: my father's voice.

Laura Marshall

A Quality Father

*Character is a by-product;
it is produced in the great manufacture
of daily duty.*

—Woodrow Wilson

Life was pure and uncomplicated growing up in the 1950s in rural California. I can recall summer days that would last forever, a white, one-room schoolhouse with a bell tower, and a home life full of love, fun and adventure. Our family lived on 10 acres of ranch-style property, where my father owned and operated his own agricultural business.

My father was a man of contrasts and fine qualities. His personality could change from comic to brusque, but he always had a heart of gold. He could carve a toothpick or a bed frame, make a dollhouse or build a church in primitive Fiji. He was talented enough to make fine silver jewelry or construct vehicles huge enough to run on a railroad. My father was a man before his time with hopes, visions and dreams he shared with our mother and his four children.

We were poor, and we struggled financially for many years. Yet, even with the endless hours our father put into his business, he still found time to invest in his children. He was available and involved in our day-to-day activities, and included us in his work as well. Educating us was one of his greatest pleasures—teaching us about history, the future, entertainment, culture, foods and advertising (one of his pet peeves).

He would often laugh at advertisements on billboards, on the radio or on television. He always had an opinion. When the ad said something was a "quality" product, he would begin a passionate dialogue, asking us rhetorical questions such as: Just what kind of quality are they talking about? Is it a product of poor, good or excellent quality? Does quality mean anything all by itself?

These days I think of those comments when people refer to "quality time" with their children and others they love. It's difficult to schedule love and special moments. You can't make an appointment to share love. My father taught me that the investment of time in one's family gives life's greatest return. The quality of my life was so rich when I was growing up, I didn't realize that we were so poor. If my father were alive today, I know I could make him laugh again by telling him he was a "quality father"!

Winnifred Comfort

A Natural Man

*I always prefer to believe the best of everybody—
it saves so much trouble.*

—Rudyard Kipling

"Don't talk to strangers," parents warn their children. This is good advice, but I grew up differently. My daddy didn't bring it up because he talked to strangers all the time—it was as natural as breathing for him. Whether he was sitting or standing, waiting for someone to come or something to happen, he would find a nondenominational, unthreatening way to start a conversation. "Do you live around here?" he would sometimes say. The heat, the cold, the rain—just about anything—made a good starting place. I watched, listened and remembered.

He told me about other things, like growing up on a red clay farm in northern Georgia. One of 12 children, he went to school through the third grade. By then he was big enough to work in the fields. Later, when the time came for him to go out on his own, he took the train to Florida. He had hoped to go to Texas to live with an aunt there, but he didn't have enough money for the ticket. In Florida he found work in the budding orange growing business. Later, he and a cousin, using borrowed money, cleared 10 acres of virgin hammock land near the head of the Indian River and planted an orange grove.

This happened before 1920; chain saws and bulldozers had not been invented. All the rope-like vines, prickly-edged palmettos, giant oaks and pines were cut and cleared using only axes, saws and fire. Snakes, skunks, opossums and even bears were never far away. Worst of all were the hordes of mosquitoes that bred in the shallow waters nearby. This personal encounter with nature at its toughest increased Daddy's respect and appreciation for the relationship between man and nature. It influenced his thinking and his philosophy, as it does for most people who live and work close to the land.

As time passed and I grew older, Daddy would talk to me about how I should behave. "Be natural," he would say. "Be yourself. Don't try to imitate somebody else or be something you aren't." These conversations frequently took place in his little black pickup truck. He would drive me home from high school when I stayed late for drama practice or club meetings. During the five-mile drive home we covered many subjects, including his thoughts about friends and companions. "You are judged by the company you keep," he would say. Most of all he impressed upon me the importance of not "putting on airs." He would see an older woman, her wrinkled face framed by coal-black hair, and say, "that's not natural."

Because of Daddy, I've never colored my hair. So when I go into a store, salespeople look at my white hair, and figure my brain is old and washed out, too. I guess they think I don't know what I want. My 75-year-old friends with dyed hair get much better service than I do.

I try to be natural and be myself, as Daddy said. But most of all I make it a point to speak to strangers. In these uncertain times, with many troubled people on the streets, I must use more caution and judgment in approaching people, but the world can be a lonely place without reaching out to others. They wait for an outstretched hand, a friendly word. Thanks to my daddy's example, I don't hesitate to speak to strangers. It comes naturally to me.

Virginea Dunn Cooper

The Role Model

Little boys are odd,
tiresome creatures in many ways,
with savage instincts; and I suppose that many
fathers feel that, if they are to maintain
their authority, they must be a little
distant and inscrutable.

—A. C. Benson

Like so many fathers in the 1950s, mine lived on the outskirts of our family. He worked a lot, traveled at times and didn't have much to say when he was home. Mom was the garrulous parent. She discussed our day, put Band-Aids on our cuts and lavished praise on our finger paintings.

During the summer Dad would occasionally dig out a flat old baseball glove and play catch with his three sons. Sometimes he'd drive us all to the beach. When we were little, my two brothers and I once took turns tickling my father as he dozed on the sofa. Without opening his eyes, Dad made a game of trying to catch us with a swooping hand as we screamed, giggled and dashed out of reach. But that sort of thing is rare in my memory. I just don't remember a whole lot about Dad during my childhood. To me he felt present but not accounted for.

This wasn't what I had in mind for a father. What I had in mind was a guy who took up more space. Someone who could hit home runs, stare down the bad guys, was handy with a hammer and with his fists. At an age when bullies were picking on me, I wanted a role model—someone to imitate when it came time to stick up for myself. I'd been hoping for Superman but had to settle for mild-mannered Clark Kent.

But once in a while Dad surprised us.

When I was seven we were at a museum in Chicago that had a full-sized car simulator. My older brother and I couldn't wait to try it out. But a potbellied guard brushed us aside. "Too small," he bellowed. He then helped a comely blonde get behind the wheel and showed her how to steer.

My father went over and talked to the guard. Dad spoke so softly that I had trouble catching his words, but thought I heard, "There was no need for you to be rude to my children." I was shocked. My dad was sticking up for his kids! But that's the only such incident I can remember.

Being a member of my family made us easy prey for little Lex Luthors. With a soft-spoken father and an older brother who was regularly chased home from school by the Doyle brothers, I resolved early on never to run from a fight. And I didn't. I lost a lot of skirmishes, but I set myself apart from my family. This became the theme of my childhood: letting the world know that at least one of my father's sons would put up his dukes.

While growing up, the cornerstone of my identity consisted of *not* being the man my father was. He was usually late; I was always prompt. Dad never fought; I often did. He was soft-spoken; I raised my voice. As the years passed, however, my guard has dropped. Now I have trouble being on time. People frequently ask me to speak up. Accepting any and all invitations to fight has come to seem more stupid than manly, even though avoiding conflict puts me in danger of feeling like the chicken I'd imagined my father to be.

But Dad no longer seems to be quite the pushover I thought he was. He didn't change—my attitude did. So did my under-standing of him. In our talks I discovered that my father once traveled halfway across the country to help his sister deal with her abusive husband, first taking care to find the man's pistol, break it down and hide the parts. On his own initiative Dad later picketed a whites-only barbershop all by himself. When fired as an economics professor by Penn State (partially due to his political beliefs), he took part in a protest by students and colleagues, which won him reinstatement. And, in a temporary lapse from pacifism, my father was ready to kill Nazis, although his gaunt six-foot, 130-pound frame kept him out of the service.

As Dad grew older it became easier for us to talk. It turned out that my father had a lot to say. Or perhaps I was just listening better. As I learned more about him, I began to see my father differently. I noticed the devotion of his friends—men and women of all ages.

"Your dad is one of my favorites," the man who handles his medical claims once told me. "Did you know that he wrote a poem for me?"

His friends see something in my father I have sometimes overlooked: not just a gentle good nature but an integrity that goes down to the bone. Over time, my own perspective has changed. The mildness I'd mistaken for passivity came to look more like quiet self-possession.

My father was a basically uncomplicated person. There was no difference that I can detect between his inner and outer self. He had difficulty sustaining a conversation with his grandchildren, just as he had trouble talking with his children. Kid talk was not my father's strong suit. That was part of his integrity. He talked the same way to everyone. Dad did nothing for effect, partly because this would have violated his sense of honor, partly because he just didn't know how. He lacked guile.

I wish that were more true of me. I have different faces for different situations and have cut ethical corners. Someone once asked me what type of man my father was. Without thinking, I responded, "He's high quality. I wish I had half his quality."

Our relationship grew easier over the years. In time, it felt like friendship. Dad called me to discuss his poetry, what kind of car to buy and whether or not he should remarry. When together, we sometimes sat quietly. There are few people in the world with whom I'm that comfortable. We never got too good at hugs and kisses and "I love you's," but we did the best that we could. It turns out that my father *was* the model I always wanted.

Ralph Keyes

A Constant Search

The search went on and on, the constant search
In answer to the whisper deep inside
That somewhere in the world he lived,
That perhaps he had not died.
Oh, loneliness of childhood,
Reaching for the hand that was not there,
The love of father's heart and child's heart to share!

—Margo Marshall-Olmstead

All I know of my father was told to me by my mother. I have no memory of his face except from faded photographs. Growing up from the age of three without the physical presence of a father brought its own loneliness and longing for the nearness that my friends enjoyed with their fathers.

Strolling alone on the shore of the South Esk River, which flows into the North Sea on the east coast of Scotland, I would sometimes ask myself, "What would it be like to have a father?" Would he be happy if I gathered sea shells for him, or would he walk with me on the beach and we'd pick them up together? Would he love the sound of the North Sea roaring on its tumultuous way, or would he comfort me as I expressed my fear of it? Fathers are never afraid, are they? When he was a young lad playing on the same beach had he wondered, as I did, if the seagulls felt free when they spread their wings and soared up to the clouds, or if they worried about their fledglings below learning to fly?

Visiting friends' homes where fathers lived, I would sense the presence of a "man's world" that filled the air: the strong scent of Lifebuoy soap, pipe smoke or cigar ashes; big boots perched on the hearth drying out for morning; soft, warm slippers waiting by the footstools for a father's feet to slide into them and relax for the evening.

As my sisters and brother and I sat around our mother's knee, she would speak of our father. "A very gentle person he was," she would say, "but also adventurous."

From the age of 14, when he joined the British Army, his courage and determination took him far from his native shores to fight for freedom and fairness—as strong men have for generations. First he was sent to India, and later to Africa to fight in the Boer War.

Love of music, too, was part of him—an ear in fact so attuned to sound that it led him to the study of how others spoke. The native dialects of India and Africa so enchanted him that he was awarded a medal as an interpreter in Pushtu and other languages.

He also had a keen sense of humor and made others happy with his friendly personality. He told of how his regiment, the Gordon Highlanders, properly dressed in their Scottish kilts, scared the enemy. When confronted by these men in "skirts" led by the skirl of the bagpipes, the natives scattered in retreat.

The years have passed, but he's still part of me. I am still part of him and always will be. I have always missed the nearness of him. Yet, his love, determination, optimism, courage, gentleness and humor live within my heart.

Margo Marshall-Olmstead

Perseverance

*I watched a small man with thick
calluses on both hands work 15 hours a day. . . .
a man who came here uneducated, alone,
unable to speak the language, who taught me all
I needed to know about faith and hard work
by the simple eloquence of example.*

**—Mario Cuomo
speaking about his father**

As a child growing up in the shadows of steel mills that sur-rounded my hometown of Pittsburgh, I received a continuing education from my parents on the importance of "sticking with something" once I began. It didn't matter what the chore or the project was—from polishing my shoes for school to getting an A in history.

My father set the example for me. He was from the old school. To him, if something was worth doing, it was worth doing right. The principles of honesty, steadfastness and dogged determination were inherent in him.

In a harsh climate, the winter of 1953 was especially brutal. Snow began to fall around Thanksgiving, and there was snow on the ground until after Easter. During one blizzard, the city was paralyzed. The temperature dropped to 20 degrees below zero, with a howling, freezing wind. Public transportation came to a halt, and the few hardy souls who attempted to drive often ended up in 10-foot-deep snowdrifts.

My father arose as usual that bleak, cold morning. We were all astonished when he announced that he intended, as he did every day, to go to work.

"I'll walk," he announced. "It's only eight miles, and I'll bundle up."

"You'll catch your death," my mother protested. "Don't be so stubborn."

Despite her pleas and the concern on the faces of his children, Dad went out the door that morning, up the icy road and into the whiteness that blanketed everything in sight. Somehow, he made it to his job at U.S. Steel that morning, and he worked a full day. There was hardly anyone there, he said, except for a few workers who lived close to the mill.

When he got home that night, he was shaking with cold. The fatigue and strain were evident in his eyes. We watched him slowly remove his snow-covered boots and the heavy woolen socks that were soaked through. With a great sigh of relief, he leaned back in his favorite chair with the worn plaid upholstery. My mother handed him a cup of steaming hot beef broth she had been simmering for hours. She scolded him again for going out in the storm and risking his health.

With a steady gaze and a quiet voice, Dad said, "You don't understand. I had to go. It's my job."

I don't know if it's perseverance or a work ethic that's almost disappeared. All I know is that my father was a deeply religious man; somehow he found the strength from within to do what he thought was right. I believe we can all find this strength under the most terrible circumstances, if we surrender our will to God. My father must have had his help that day.

Margaret A. McDonald

Gallant Arnie

*What lies behind us and what lies before us
are tiny matters compared with
what lies within us.*

—**Source unknown**

By the time I met my father-in-law, Arnie, I had already formed
some pretty bitter opinions about husbands and fathers. My father
had walked out when I was 10 years old, and I was raised by my
mother (a fantastic woman from whom I learned volumes about
grit and determination). I obviously did not look forward to marriage as a safe haven or the answer to girlhood dreams.

Nevertheless, I married too young and had my first child when
I was 17. Like many teen marriages, mine ended within two years.
With it went a large chunk of my already shaky self-esteem and
what was left of my faith in men. I resigned myself to the fact that
not only do men not contribute—they leave.

In 1978, when my son, Kevin, was three, I met Rory. He will
agree that I wasn't the easiest person to get close to, but there
was an instant chemistry between us. Before I knew it, he was
taking me to meet his parents.

Arnie and Mayme were sitting at the kitchen table visiting with
Rory's aunt and uncle when we arrived. Introductions were made,
coffee was poured and the kitchen erupted in lively conversation.

I was entertained with stories of my future husband's boyhood antics and athletic victories, complete with scrapbooks and photo albums Mayme had carefully assembled. As we were chatting, Kevin slipped down off my lap. When I turned to see where he was going, I saw that Arnie, too, had ducked out and was on the floor of the adjoining room, setting up the pieces of a magnetic football game. Arnie gave me a reassuring smile, and I turned to rejoin the conversation while he and Kevin passed the time playing football.

As I got to know Rory and his family better, I heard stories of Arnie's commitment and devotion to his wife and children that softened even my hard heart. I learned, for instance, that when their first two children were young, Mayme fell victim to polio. Doctors told them that she would surely never walk again and would not be able to have any more children. Although I knew her as a determined woman, I'm sure that Arnie's love and support contributed greatly to her ability to defy the doctor's predictions and not only walk again, but also give birth to their third child—my husband.

Arnie filled many roles as Mayme fought to regain her strength during those years. And I'm sure that he never considered himself heroic or gallant. He was just doing what good men do: caring for his family.

Eventually it was back to life as usual for Arnie and Mayme and their young family. Arnie was so dedicated to his children, and spent so much time coaching and working with kids in his community, that he was honored as Citizen of the Year in their hometown in Washington state.

I also learned that back in the '60s their teenage daughter's rebellion had landed her scared and alone near the infamous street corner of Haight-Ashbury in San Francisco. She called home, and Arnie did what a good dad does—he drove across three states to bring her back home where she belonged.

When their oldest son served in Vietnam, Arnie, like thousands of other fathers in America, spent many sleepless nights praying for his son's safe return.

These stories of unconditional love and commitment were unbelievable to me. But when Rory and I were married, I learned first-hand of the full extent of Arnie's thoughtfulness and generosity.

Our first home was low on price and high on potential, a real "fixer-upper," and Arnie didn't wait to be asked. He loaned tools, trucks and money. He spent many weekends pounding nails, pulling wires and patching chimneys. For the first time in my life, I began to understand what it felt like to have a father I could depend on to be there for me no matter what.

Rory and I soon had two more boys and began the whirlwind we all know as family life. Over the years, I've seen Arnie rock babies, cheer on Little Leaguers, fix bicycles, fill gas tanks, deliver surplus garden vegetables, build campfires, carve turkeys, settle arguments and sit in the rain on graduation day.

Retired, with their children grown and grandchildren sprouting up everywhere, it seemed Arnie and Mayme's lives would find an easy pace. But their good fortune and good marriage would be tested once again. In 1984, Mayme was diagnosed with breast cancer, and she began treatment immediately. Through it all, Arnie was the voice of calm optimism. He accompanied her on visits to the doctor, waited nervously while she underwent surgery and reassured her as the disease became visible in her appearance.

Later, when we learned that her cancer had spread and was becoming more than even this strong woman could endure, Arnie never left her side.

He administered medicine, cooked meals, comforted and encouraged. Their dream of spending their retirement years traveling the Southwest together ended on June 26, 1986. Arnie spent some time grappling with the questions and grief of Mayme's death but remained remarkably strong. His ability to move forward was, I believe, the legacy of having done the right thing for 40 years.

Later, a wonderful, energetic and artistic woman came into Arnie's life. With her encouragement, he has awakened within himself an artistic talent and love for painting that he never knew existed. They spend their winters in the Southwest, and when they are home, they spend their days painting the images they bring back. Being the wonderful husband that he is, he has held his new wife's hand through illness and comforted her during times of loss in her family.

Arnie has given me a priceless gift just by doing what he considers normal. By standing by his wife and being there for his children and grandchildren, he has restored my faith and taught me that sometimes men *don't* leave.

Fortunately for me, they also raise sons who don't leave.

Laurel Turner

My Hero

Here I sit cross-legged
on the window seat,
my Mary Jane shoes covered
tentlike by my dress.
I am like a dog that senses
when the children will return from school,
only this is more exciting.
I will see him when he turns the corner
two doors down.
Yes, there he comes!

I know he is happy—
absentmindedly whistling
his happy tune,
"Marching Through Georgia."
And soon
Daddy swoops me up,
my Buster Brown haircut flying up
as I come back down to earth
giggling.

After our noon dinner
he kisses my mother on the cheek
and eases into his chair,
the foot of his crossed leg
almost touching the floor;
and I hop on his ankle
for an after-dinner horsey ride.
As he reads the *Grand Rapids Press,*
I play with my box "desk"
behind his chair,
filing the sample forms
he has brought me
from his newspaper office.

A smoke signal
from his walking-to-work cigar
sends me skipping to his side.
We walk to the corner,
my tiny hand enveloped by his,
and looking way up
I see that smile
and the twinkle in his eyes
that says we share a secret—
a secret we never had to tell each other,
we just knew.

Jane Mayes

Daredevil Dad

Unrest of spirit is a mark of life.

—Karl Menninger

Once upon a time—just a few months ago really—I viewed my life as a road that would go on forever, a road without doctors that would carry me, aboard my motorcycle, through an extended adolescence that stretched farther than I could see.

I loved to pack a change of clothes, some camping gear, and a fly rod and camera, hop onto my bike, and disappear for a day or a week, leaving the details of business in a cloud of exhaust. My favorite destination was anywhere I hadn't been. Until recently, a daylong ride down a two-lane country road—then pitching my tent by a clear, trouty river and naming constellations until I drifted into sleep—was as good as life gets. In the morning, there would be wake-up coffee to sip in a roadside cafe, and overalled locals to chat with who would want to know, "Where you been on that thing?" Then I'd be off, happily connecting the dots on the road.

But that was before Alice.

I picked up my first pair of blended bifocals and learned I would become a father—for the first time—on my 45th birthday. At that age, I thought I had bypassed my child-rearing years. I had accepted that children were not, and would not be, a part of my life. But my wife is 15 years younger and . . . Alice just happened.

101

Hey, here's Alice now, squirming on the changing table as I get her dressed. I lean in to touch noses with her, something that delights us both. I inhale deeply, filling my lungs with Essence of Alice. Nothing—not baking bread, not even the pungent smell of a motorcycle shop—is as intoxicating as the scent of this baby. I want to protect my child, the source of this wonderful smell. I surrender to the deep need to shelter her, to keep her from harm. Now that she is on the verge of crawling, I worry about her bumping her head on the tabletops in our home. Should I outfit the tables with foam bumpers? Or should I outfit Alice with a crash helmet? Then I am struck by the incongruity between the need to protect Alice and the risk I take on a motorcycle.

What happens now, Alice, I ask the wind, now that I have you, and you have me? You're going to make me responsible, aren't you, Alice? What do I do now . . . spring for a new helmet? New tires? More life insurance? Do I take that motorcycle-safety class I keep putting off?

And how do I prepare myself for the day that Alice rides into the driveway on her own motorcycle, blips the throttle, and says, "Hop on, Dad, let's go for a ride." What then? Will I deny Alice the same freedom, the same sensations, I claim for myself?

There are inherent risks in riding a motorcycle; there's no arguing that point. No motorcyclist has ever gotten the best of a pickup truck that turned into his path. No rider ever limped away from a lay-down without a glistening case of road rash. How about that time in Taos, I remind myself, early in the morning, when I was hurrying to rendezvous with friends, and that red-eyed guy in the Chevy was zoned out in the middle of the road with no brake lights? The adrenaline, the skid, the recovery, the quick lane change—a close call. For all the fun and freedom that motorcycling provides, it is ultimately unforgiving of mistakes.

It's one thing to risk my own life, but now that I am a motorcyclist who is also a father, I have a responsibility to view my life through a different pair of eyes, the eyes of my child.

I search for the answer in Alice's eyes and try to imagine what she might say if we shared a common language. Would she prefer that I do my adventuring in front of the TV? Or complete my vagabonding years from the cockpit of a minivan? Maybe she would suggest that I take up something less risky, like golf. Or perhaps she would want me to continue to enjoy motorcycling, but to sharpen my skills and learn how to minimize and manage the risks involved.

Then she reaches up, touches my beard and coos—a very distinct two-syllable coo. What's that, Alice? What did you say? There it is again, as clear and focused as the desert after a rain: "Ride safe, Dad."

Those dark eyes are constant reminders that I am no longer riding alone, or at my own risk. I have a passenger now, a little girl whose spirit rides with me every mile. Now she wraps her chubby fingers around my finger and squeezes, as if it were a throttle.

"Hold on, Alice," I tell her. "Life is a wonderful adventure. You're going to love it."

Dale Smith

Reprinted from the July 1992 issue of *Parents* magazine.

A Man of Few Words

*Silence is a true friend
who never betrays.*

—Confucius

My father had an unvarying ritual when he returned from work late at night, when we were all asleep. We lived in what was then called a railroad flat on the Upper East Side of Manhattan. When my father returned home in the early hours of the morning from his job at the Western Electric plant in Hoboken, New Jersey, he would sit in the kitchen, a soft light from a shaded lamp on the shelf above the sink illuminating the space. We all knew that was his ritual, though the 12 of us weren't awake at one or two in the morning. Dad's life was a solemn, serious puzzle to us. Any scrap of information we gathered— either from him or from our mother—was laden with significance.

That's how it was for me when I was 12 years old. I assume my brothers and sisters felt that same longing for some contact with and understanding of this man who would wake up for work when we were at school and come home when we were in bed.

Dad had to read the *Daily News* each night. Even though he had little formal education, he was an intelligent man who prided himself on his ability to do word puzzles like the Jumble. After a beer or two, he found solace in his quiet corner doing mental exercises that challenged him more than his grueling, mindless job as a merchandise checker. These days his job is no doubt called "quality control" and requires an M.B.A.

I wanted to please my father more than anything. If I couldn't please him, I at least wanted to get his attention. But it was difficult because he was rarely home during the week. On weekends, he was irritable or distracted, and we learned to leave him alone. Now I realize how much of that behavior was just part of his nature. He was brooding, undemonstrative, solitary.

Twelve-year-old girls (and probably boys) are obviously not equipped to take that into account when they need to have some gesture of love or approval from a father. I know I wasn't. I longed to make a connection with this phantom who sat in that quiet corner each night, earnestly working on the Jumble until weariness overtook him.

I knew that he liked baseball because he listened to the games on the radio. Every now and then, my mother and father would go to the movies together while my older sister and I baby-sat. I remember how it pleased me to see them walking together. As I leaned on the sill of the living-room window, I could watch them walk toward First Avenue and the old Monroe movie theater on Seventy-Sixth Street. I felt proud of them because they were so good-looking together, and I knew it was because of my big sister and me that they were able to go off and, possibly, have some fun together.

To this day I don't know if they really had any fun together. Raising 12 children doesn't leave much time for frivolity. But those few occasions when my mother and father went out all dressed up made me believe they were happy to be together. And since I was partly responsible for making my father happy, it followed that he was pleased with me. He didn't say it, but it was enough for me that somewhere in his heart he felt it.

One day, I decided it was possible to communicate with my father. The way to do it, I realized, was to leave him a note or message on the sink, along with his newspaper. This inspiration was the simple solution to approaching a man who was always out of reach. It came to me on the day I received straight A's on my report card. My name was to be placed on the honor roll at

Richard Kelly Junior High School, and I just knew my Dad respected that kind of achievement. He didn't read books, or discuss deep philosophical issues, or have more than a high-school education (if that), but I knew he was very smart and thought about many things he didn't express.

One night, with great excitement, I left my report card with a note attached to it that said: "Dear Dad, I thought you would like to see this." I wrote it numerous times so the penmanship would be perfect. When I awoke the next morning for school, I searched the sink top for my father's reply. My heart sank as I saw my note, undisturbed, still clipped to the report card. I wondered if I had done the wrong thing by intruding upon his solitude and quiet time. But when I picked up the note, I was overjoyed. There was a response. In a tremulous, faint script made with a blunt pencil, it read: "Very Good."

My father passed away over 15 years ago, but I still feel the intense pride and joy those two words evoked in me. That first, tentative invasion of his privacy also marked the beginning of a dialogue with my father that continued for several years. When I had something important to say to him, I'd leave him a note, then eagerly look for his response the next day. He never disappointed me, though he rarely wrote more than a few words in reply. There was always some acknowledgment, and that was enough. I knew he cared for me.

My father helped me understand that sometimes the most powerful emotions render us speechless; that there is sometimes little correlation between what we say and what we feel. Have you ever noticed, in fact, how easy it is to find the words to say something when your emotions are not involved? How glib we can be when it's small talk, when the heart isn't involved.

My father, so closed and private, taught me about the eloquence of silence.

Joan Aho Ryan

Off My Father's Cuff

Wit is a glorious treat, like caviar;
never spread it about like marmalade.

—Noel Coward

A few months ago I was asked to give a speech at the New York club where my father was not only president but was known for his urbanity and wit when called upon to speak. Suspecting that many of his old friends would be in the audience, I wanted to make a special effort, not so much to enjoin a comparison as to do his memory proud.

So I called my mother, who this year celebrated her 90th birthday, for advice. She thought a folder from my father's effects titled "Speech Anecdotes" might be helpful, and she sent it over. It turned out to be a treasure trove. There, covered in my father's somewhat cramped hand, was a thick sheaf of papers torn from small pads and fastened with large paper clips. It brought back a faint unease, seeing that familiar handwriting; it reminded me of the scores of letters he wrote when I was having trouble away at school, which was almost all the time. His advice, along with the admonitions, handwritten with never a word crossed out or changed despite the complexity of the sentences, arrived in flurries at the school post office.

I leafed through the jokes, the quips, the jottings, and I decided to offer a large number of them to my audience; after all, if things didn't work out, the blame could be shared!

As I started making my selections, a portrait of my father began to emerge. It occurred to me that someone working in the depths of the CIA with my father's folder could come up with a fairly accurate composite. From the plethora of legal references, obviously he was a lawyer. "Mahatma Gandhi a lawyer? I thought from his dress that he was a client." Or, "Nixon looks like a lawyer, the other side's lawyer." The operative could assume my father was often called upon to speak in public: "I'm sorry (remarking on a flowery introduction) that you didn't mention my humility." Or, "I'm reminded of the drunk who on coming home and falling down remarked, 'I'm going to put aside my prepared remarks and answer questions from the floor.'"

My father often criticized me for spending so much time reading the sports pages, so it brought a smile to my face to come across the following: "Sports fan to political activist: 'What do you think of the Indianapolis 500?' Activist: 'They're innocent.'" On the other hand, a number of the more pragmatic jottings gave me the same twinge of inadequacy I felt in those early schoolboy days when I opened his letters: "If at first you don't succeed, try, try again, then quit. No use being a damn fool about it—W.C. Fields."

A couple of entries suggested that he was getting on in age: "No one is old until he starts being proud of his age." Or this: "By the time you have money to burn, the fire is out."

Of course, some of what I turned up would have puzzled the CIA operative in his warren—items from Father's reading that simply tickled his fancy: "Monotonous monogamy is pernicious polygamy." Or a phrase from Rebecca West's *Black Lamb and Grey Falcon:* "The grey ice that forms on an Englishman's face when introduced to a stranger."

The closest approach to scatology was a story of a diplomat about to address a large audience of Russians in Moscow, whom he hoped to impress by starting off, "Ladies and gentlemen" in their language. He did so, but could tell from the startled looks down in front that something had gone badly amiss. Later, he discovered that the signs on the restroom doors had been an unfortunate source. He had started off his speech: "Toilets and urinals . . ."

I didn't bring that particular story to the club because I knew my mother would be in the audience; she shies away from such references. But I had a long list of the others. I rattled them off, Gatling-gun style, one after another. That was pretty much the body of my talk. It went well, I thought. Occasionally, there were nods of recognition—oh, yes, that one. One of Father's former friends, a fellow lawyer, approached me later in the club's library. He said he had borrowed a few quips from Father's speeches and believed Father had borrowed the Mahatma Gandhi from him many years before.

My mother was somewhat surprised by the volume of material. She thought I would extract only two or three items to pep up my talk, as Father would have done. "My goodness," she said, "I never thought I'd hear them all at once!"

George Plimpton

Deeds Speak Louder Than Words

The heart would have no rainbow
had the eyes no tears.

—Source unknown

Daddy was born in a time when it was not considered manly to say "I love you" or to cry—even when a situation desperately called for tears. Daddy would probably have lived longer had he allowed himself to cry, rather than let the unshed tears overflow inside. But he had his own way of letting us know we were loved and treasured.

The family Bible was kept in a place of honor in the parlor, on a hand-hewn table where it was easily accessible. It was large and heavy, the leather soft and worn, and it gathered no dust. Its gilded edges were the only gold we ever knew, and its purple ribbon gave us a touch of kinship to royalty. But the fascinating part of this Bible were the pages between the Old and New Testaments.

This is where the marriages, births and deaths were recorded. On the pages titled "Births," in his fine Spencerian script, my father recorded with pride the full name and birth date of each of his 12 children.

With his callused farmer's hands, he would pick up a toddler and set her on his knee. From the bib pocket of his faded blue overalls, he took a watch he had carried since his youth. A touch to the winding stem and the top sprang open. He held it to the child's ear, and she held her breath as she listened to the barely audible tick . . . tick . . . tick. Holding it carefully with its attached chain between his fingers, and with the watch itself cradled in the palm of his hand, he used its face to teach us the Roman numerals and "a quarter after" and "half past" the hour.

Sitting in a rocking chair on the high front porch that provided a peaceful scene of Beaver Creek and the fields beyond, he held his pipe with one hand and pressed the child to his breast with the other. The child felt warm and safe, and the rhythmic beat of his heart lulled her to sleep while he smoked his pipe and relaxed in the cool of the evening.

As we walked through the orchard, he would pull a sheepnose apple from the tree, polish it to a high shine on the sleeve of his blue chambray shirt, hand it to the child and exhort, with his own peculiar one-sided grin, "An apple a day keeps the doctor away."

Jack, a medium-sized thoroughbred collie, had been his constant companion for 16 years—since the day he brought the pup home as a gift from a favorite uncle. But Jack grew old and could no longer bring the cows in from the field at milking time or protect our home at night from possible intruders. We children could not understand why Jack could no longer run and play in the fields with us. Age had taken its toll on Jack. He was nearly toothless, his frame gaunt and covered with wiry thin fur instead of the soft brown and white waves of his younger years. He awakened to eat a few bites of bread softened in milk, then slept again.

Daddy loved the dog and hated to watch him die slowly. Late one afternoon, he shouldered his rifle and walked with Jack at his heels toward the back of the barn. We children, sensing what was about to happen, silently said good-bye to Jack and sat quietly as we awaited Daddy's return.

Time passed slowly, and our eyes searched the horizon. Later, he returned with the tired dog at his heels, hung the rifle back on the nails over the hall door and said, "I couldn't do it." It was the first time we children ever saw tears in his eyes.

I have taught my own son that it is an admirable trait to say "I love you." I have told him that it's okay to cry when crying is called for and that hugs are healthy. My daddy, who kept it all within, has made me realize how important this is.

Mary B. Ledford

Truths My Father
Never Told Me

You are what you are when nobody is looking.

—Abigail Van Buren

My father was a tobacco-chewing carpenter, a man with a sixth-grade education, not the best sense of syntax or grammar, and I spent much of my life being ashamed of him. After all, he had false teeth, rough hands so ingrained with dirt that they never approached looking clean, and he never read anything more serious than the daily newspaper. I knew there was something more to life than the East Side of Cleveland, Ohio, and what later was called "blue collar" work, but I was equally certain that this man was not fit to be my guide into the larger world, of which I so badly wanted to be part. Before I understood what the term "role model" meant, he was out of the running.

I didn't want my friends to meet him and hear subjects that never consulted their predicates. I'd always manage to be waiting in the driveway to be picked up. When I went to college and my fellow freshmen told me their fathers were "in" something like real estate or accounting or sales, my father suddenly was "in construction."

He wasn't a notable father in even the most rudimentary sense. I played three sports in grade school, but he never saw a game, never gave me a ride or told me he was proud it was my basket that beat St. Margaret's or my tackle that held Holy Rosary at the goal line. There was never to be that wonderful after-game scene with father walking toward the station wagon, arm draped over the huge shoulder pads that for an afternoon made his boy almost a man, confiding, "It's not who wins or loses, Son, but how you . . ."

He didn't teach me to catch a ball or encourage me to play sports, nor did he urge me on to college, or in any way urge me to better myself. He never lectured me, never *told* me anything. We never had a direct conversation, much less a heart-to-heart talk, so that I could learn what it was I needed to take along on a life's journey.

After all, he was just a working man who'd come through the Depression, sired and raised seven children, suffered the indignities of standing on food lines and having a house he'd built with those dirt-grimed hands taken away because he couldn't pay the few dollars of taxes. He stopped for a shot and a beer every night after work. Obviously, he had no wisdom or insights to impart from such an undistinguished life.

He's been dead some 15 years now, but as every Father's Day comes around, I find myself thinking about him and what he did give me. It took me so long to understand the man and his worth. This year I asked myself: What did I learn from him that I want to pass on to my two sons? I came up with a modest list—of attitudes, really, about work and detachment, generosity and rage, and about square corners, that most central issue in every man's life.

Work: He always got to the job before the other men who worked for the small construction company that employed him for 20 years. And he often was the last to leave, mumbling something under his breath about "Some bastard'll knock that over fer sure" as he shored up a side wall or nailed the last window casing in place. Did he do it for overtime pay or to impress the boss? Hardly.

"A man pay you fer eight hours work, you do nine," he'd say, not with any special pride, but simply because it was what an honest workingman did. It was an honor to be employed, a gift, and in his own way he acknowledged that every day.

Detachment: He never criticized me when I almost flunked out of college, and he never really congratulated me when my stories began to appear in a good number of national magazines. As emphysema, fed by coal dust in Pennsylvania and sawdust in Cleveland, gradually suffocated him, forcing him to spend his days at our worn breakfast-nook table, he'd take deep, wheezing breaths and pat a pile of dog-eared publications at his side. "I dunno; I guess Butch (he never once called me Paul) got some stories in 'em." It was as close as he would ever come to encouraging someone to read something I'd written, as he had obviously done many times.

Generosity: With a mother-in-law (whom he detested), a wife and seven kids to support, he earned barely enough to cover our needs, but my father always felt that there was more than enough to go around. You had only to appear at our house anywhere close to mealtime, and he would insist you be fed. Roast beef or cornmeal mush: if we had it, you had it. If my father passed up seconds, saying he wasn't that hungry, it was one of the few times he might lie. And, if you came after five o'clock weekdays and anytime on Saturday or Sunday, you'd be confronted with a frighteningly large shot glass of Corby's whiskey and a bottle of Erin Brew. The man was poor, but he never thought of himself as poor.

A Just Rage: He was usually a mild-mannered man who worked quietly and never complained, even when his boss gave him the dirtiest, most odious part of one of their "fire jobs," reconstructing a burned-out store or residence. But when he got home too late and too woozy on Friday night, and my mother counted out a slightly depleted pay envelope, he could be relied upon to put her in her place. "I beat my brains out all day and if I can't stop fer a little . . ." He would take abuse on the job, sometimes the scorn of his family, but when a certain point was reached, my father would rise up in righteous indignation and reclaim his dignity.

Square Corners: To watch him at work was to see a master carpenter. He seldom missed a nail, never gouged wood, even if it was interior framing that would soon be covered with wallboard. Corners were somehow mystically important to him, even those no one would see. I can recall him taking great pains to bevel perfectly the edges of two pieces of baseboard that would be all but hidden from view behind a huge and rather ugly radiator cover. The workday was over, and I was impatient for him to get finished, but he wouldn't do a slipshod job. "They ain't gonna know the difference, Butch, but this guy knows," he said, thumb pointing toward his chest.

How I'd like to ensure somehow that I pass along to my sons the quiet lessons that—too late in life—I realize he'd taught me. I'd like to impress upon my boys that they should work hard at something decent and honorable and not count the hours or the cost. That they should be ready not just to give from their excess, but to share graciously whatever they have.

I want them to know that to be a reflective man is to possess a great virtue and that they should walk at once tall but meek in the world, even at the risk of sometimes being considered weak. But I also want them to be sure that when the line they themselves draw is crossed, they let everyone within hearing know of it. And I would hope they learn that it is not only what shows that is the measure of the man: the principle of square corners.

I am my father's son, and I know, whether it ever was a conscious or intentional decision, that I've tried to live by those truths he never told me. But, foolish man that I am, I didn't learn well enough. I find myself talking about the dignity of work and square corners to my older son, and I'm sure I'll blab on to the younger one, too, as soon as he'll listen. My words overstate my actions. My father did it beautifully, in reverse.

How I wish my father were around now. I'd get him a tall pineapple-juice can for that Havana Blossom tobacco juice and tell my boys just to sit and watch him, hoping they might learn much more quickly than I did—from a real role model, a man who knew intuitively that before you are a great father, you are a good man.

Paul Wilkes

What I Want to Say to My Dad

Riley O'Connell wrote the following letter to her dad as part of a class assignment in Ms. Breton's seventh-grade literature class at St. Andrews School in Coral Springs, Florida.

Dear Dad,

I am writing you this letter to thank you for being you. In the past 12 years you have taught me so much. One of the things you have taught me about is business. Ever since I was four years old you would take me almost every weekend and show me what you do to get ready for lunch and dinner at your restaurants. You still take me!

You have also taught me about my Irish heritage. You have told me a lot about my relatives. You've shown me pictures and artifacts of places where they lived. You have also show me how to spend a lot of time with my family by taking me to my Uncle Paul's house every week and taking me to see my other relatives as much as possible. Wow! You busy man! Look at what you have taught me in the past 12 years! I would just like to thank you and tell you I love you!

Your daughter,
Riley

Cedric Jean-Baptiste submitted a diary entry for the same class assignment.

Dear Diary:

On April 15, 1984, as I was handed to my father, I could see the joy in his eyes. He held me and said, "Cedric, my son, I will care for you all my life." He had a hard grip on me as if he never wanted to let me go. As my tiny eyes looked into his face, I knew my dad and I would have a great relationship.

As I grew older, we bonded even closer. We went to the park, played games and had lots of fun together.

After the passing of my mother, we held each other closely, like the day I was born. But when I looked into his eyes, they were not the eyes of joy. They were the eyes of sadness. The joy in his eyes came down with the tears, and from that point on I knew it was not going to be like old times anymore. We are still bonded, but not as well as before.

He likes it when I work hard, and when I do, I see a little joy in his eyes again. Like old times, he says, "That's my boy," and I stand proud.

One day, when I get older, he will give me those eyes of joy so that I may pass them down to my children. And when he dies, I will kneel on his grave, and I will say the words he always wanted me to say to him: "Thanks, Dad."

The Tank

*A master can tell
you what he expects of you.
A teacher, though, awakens your
own expectations.*

—Patricia Neal

My father gave me a gift that has shaped my entire adult life, although I didn't realize it until recently. The story about this gift begins with my brother, Gary, who is four years younger than I. Until I became a teenager, we played together every day. We defended a fort made of chairs and sheets. We played Let's Make a Deal. Gary was Monte Hall and I the lovely Carol Merrill. And we played doctor until Gary amputated the ears from all the stuffed animals.

As I grew up, I began to show leadership qualities: patrol leader in the Girl Scouts, president of my high-school service club, director of the children's choir at church. I also got good grades in school. Gary's grades were average. My parents would often remind him that I had excellent grades and was achieving recognition. School was harder for Gary than it was for me, and he wasn't the extrovert I was.

I knew Gary was frustrated by the sibling competition—a fact that was driven home the day Gary got angry and called me a "tank." When he said it, I was insulted. After all, a tank is something that rolls over everything in its path to reach the target. That's how he meant it, and for decades, that's how I took it.

When I turned 40, I realized there was more to a tank than rolling destruction. A tank is tough, able to function in any terrain. When bombs are exploding all around, when the war is going on in front and behind, the tank moves forward purposefully toward the target. Gary was right—it was an apt description of how I move steadily toward a goal. When he visited me recently, we reminisced about how much our dad instilled this in both of us.

Gary was proud of a promotion at his firm, bragging about saving enough money to buy the sailboat he'd always dreamed of owning. What color did I think he should get? I laughed. His goal-directed behavior reminded me of all those times he called me a tank. I asked him if he remembered it. He was stunned until he realized he was enjoying his success for the same reasons he had called me a tank: confidence, focus and determination.

"Do you think it's genetic?" I asked.

"No," he said, "I think it's learned behavior. Don't you remember that Dad's basic philosophy about life was that you can do anything you put your mind to?

Can I have a new bike? Can I go with the church choir to Europe? Can I get an after-school job? His response was always the same: "You can do anything you want if you're willing to work hard enough."

He had high expectations for us. By telling us we could do anything if we only worked hard enough, Dad taught us to raise our standards for ourselves. Our dreams weren't out of reach, not if we stretched. Dreams were just goals we hadn't reached yet.

Today as a college professor, I counsel students. It is a thrill when we can dream about possibilities for their lives and plan strategies to achieve them.

For example, a senior majoring in newspaper journalism came to my office to chat. She was frustrated and scared because she realized she never wanted to be a newspaper reporter or editor. The work didn't suit her, but she couldn't afford to change majors and stay in school an extra year or two. She didn't know what other major she could choose.

I asked her where she saw herself in 5 or 10 years, and what her dreams were. She said she majored in journalism because she liked to write. But when she spoke about a career with the newspapers, her shoulders slumped, and her nose wrinkled. Yet, she sparkled when she spoke of herself wearing business attire, working in a professional environment, writing, planning events and helping other people solve problems.

"What about public relations?" I asked.

"I don't know anything about PR," she said.

So I called a couple of my friends in the PR business and arranged for her to meet them. Several weeks later, I received a note that read:

> Dear Dr. Workman:
>
> Thank you for introducing me to public relations. I love it! Nobody has ever made me feel as special as you did when you took the time to help me see opportunities instead of obstacles. I was really scared to meet the people you called, but you had so much confidence in me I knew I had to try. At first I did it for you, but after I got there, I had fun. In fact, one of the companies asked me to apply for a job! You changed my life because you believed in me. I won't be so scared to try something new next time.

My student had no idea she was thanking me for sharing my father's gift of self-esteem. When you have self-esteem, you have the confidence of a tank—focused and determined. My father built self-esteem every time he said, "You can do anything you put your mind to."

Yes, Dad, when you believe you can do it, you can do it.

Gale A. Workman

Truths My Father Taught Me

It is not truth that makes man great,
but man who makes truth great.

—Confucius

"Look, a two-headed bike!" said a child passing by. That confirmed it: on our tandem bicycle, Dad and I were invincible. Riding with Dad, I didn't think about being blind. I just did what everybody else did on the back seat of a tandem: no steering, just pedaling.

It was late spring in my quiet hometown of Bradley Beach, New Jersey. For the first time since the previous summer, there was enough light left for a bike trip after supper. We began our ride by turning east toward the boardwalk. The sun, seeming to grow more fiery as it set, swung around my cheek. Dad described the grass that was growing and that which was not, because the birds had gotten to the seed. He stopped to show me the lumber used on construction work. Over there was a clam shell that seagulls had somehow known to drop on the concrete to make it crack open. Dad wasn't just being my eyes, he was sharing every one of his perceptive, inquisitive senses.

As we approached the boardwalk, the ocean just beyond began to speak in many voices. There was, of course, the low rumble I could hear from far away. But now there was the swish of water going in and out, like a great beast inhaling and exhaling. I imagined that each wave traveled its own separate path, all the way from Europe.

Feeling adventurous, we sped over the bridge that linked the nearby towns of Avon and Belmar, the bells clanging their warning that the bridge would open soon even as we neared the top. "Pedal harder," Dad said. And just to show that he had everything in hand, he maintained top speed after our descent on the far side, jiggling the tandem past parking meters that suddenly whooshed by on our right.

The bike coming toward us was going fast, much faster than we were. For a second, I heard the hum of its tires vibrating on the boardwalk. I felt Dad swerve the tandem before he could explain to me why he was doing it. At first it seemed the other bike had just grazed our front wheel. But the collision had caused us to begin shaking. Although we kept moving forward, we were swaying more and more. Finally, we fell.

Neither one of us was hurt, and I'm sure Dad forgot about it quickly. But there was a lesson in this that Dad had not intended to teach me. For the first time in my life, I realized that my father was not invincible. Vaguely, I sensed that someday he would not be there to guide me.

As if to allay my fears about the future, Dad began spending more and more time with my mother, brother, sister and me. As his men's clothing business became more secure, we spent three or four days a week at the beach during July and August, returning home at dusk. There were surprise trips to New York. Through Dad, I toured the captain's quarters of a ferryboat and met a few of the New York Yankees.

His immense store of energy almost persuaded me that somehow he wasn't getting any older. If anything, he showed more concern for my coming of age than for his own aging. In the safety of our home, he let me experience what it was like to feel a little tipsy so that later I could say "no" with conviction to my peers. Before I ever signed a check, Dad had me convinced of the necessity of saving half a year's salary.

As I became more independent, he taught me one of his favorite decision-making criteria: "What difference will it make in 10 years?" I learned it was better to miss school for one day to keep a cold from becoming worse and okay to quit the wrestling team to join the glee club.

Later as a social-work student, I saw people the same age as Dad who had decided they didn't want to leave their homes any more. Others filled their days with pains, doctors and medicines, all described in great detail. If Dad had health problems, his children only heard about them after the cure.

I didn't learn about the spot on his lung until they were preparing him for surgery. The bicycle ride of so many years ago came to mind. The collision had happened.

I visited Dad on the eve of Yom Kippur, the time when Jews traditionally ponder God's judgment on whose names will be sealed in the Book of Life for the coming year. On the surface, Dad and I talked about recovery. But I got the sense that he, too, was feeling the collision.

Despite the pain from the operation, Dad continued to teach all of those around him. This time Mom was his student, even as she took increasing responsibility for his constant care. He taught her all the details she'd never needed to know before. As his weight dropped and his health failed, he began organizing all his papers: the insurance, the bills, the bank accounts, the monthly and quarterly and yearly obligations of all kinds.

A surgeon in Florida told him the cancer had spread to his stomach and that in all likelihood he had only a few months to live. I had the feeling he had been expecting something like this for some time. If there were anger and grief, we children were shielded from it once again. He investigated the hospice movement so he could die at home peacefully.

He put up a front for the scores of people who visited him. The conversation was always about them. Only when they went away did he admit his pain to my mother and succumb to sleep. When I visited him in December, we shared the home movies he'd preserved for us on a VCR. I was beginning to say good-bye.

By late January, he had made the final hospice arrangements, increased his intake of morphine and now only had five minutes or so every few hours during which he could communicate with anybody. He would let Mom know who it was he wanted to speak with. My sister, my brother and I, visiting at different times, waited to be summoned.

I recited the Final Confession with him. He had already made his own peace with God long before the formal prayer. "If this is Your will," he said, as it became ever harder for him to maintain himself, "I accept it."

I went in to say my final farewell. I had dreaded this moment most of all. "Good-bye for now," we both said. We were relieved that we had managed to say something. I wanted to back out of the room, the way one does from a royal presence. I wanted to make up for all those times I had not respected him. But he wouldn't have understood, so I turned and walked out slowly. "A little to your right," he said. I was not familiar with their Florida house, and as always, he was teaching me.

As I hold my son, Aharon, who bears my father's name, I think about transmitting to him the truths my father taught me. From my stories about his grandfather, Aharon will learn that those who have learned to keep their balance as they travel through life know how to end the journey with dignity.

But there is one final lesson I will explain to my son, one last teaching of my father's that lifted me through my grief and sustains me now. Though the teacher must fall, his teachings remain to steer his offspring for many generations to come.

Michael Levy

Little Hare

Perseverance is not a long race;
it is many short races, one after another.

—Walter Elliott

The most significant lesson our children learned from their father began even before they were born. The vehicle for this instruction came with four wheels and a racing stripe, and taught our family that sometimes inanimate objects speak to us with the wisdom and eloquence of Socrates.

It was early August, 1977. My fiancé, Jim, and I sat in a Shoney's in Savannah eating hot-fudge cake and debating the various merits of the new automobiles we'd seen that day. Soon we would marry and move to Florida, where Jim would begin graduate school. We needed a car.

We finally decided upon a green Volkswagen Rabbit, low-priced at $4,500. Back at the dealership, Jim's hand shook more than a little as he wrote the check that would consume almost a year's worth of his hard-earned money.

One month later, our families helped us pack up the shiny little car. Jim's sister had a parting gift—a rainbow sticker about eight inches long. In an uncharacteristic attack of whimsy, Jim peeled off the backing and plopped the vibrant rainbow dead center on the Rabbit's rear window. With a crank of the engine, we headed south, eager to begin our life together.

From the very beginning, Jim was unselfish, riding his bicycle to and from the university so that I could drive to work. One evening, when the Rabbit was about a year old, I ran a stop sign. Brakes grabbed. Tires screamed. With the sickening *bam* of colliding metal, the Rabbit rammed into another car, spun around and slammed into a tree.

Everyone was shaken but unhurt. Not so the Rabbit. As I surveyed its crushed and broken body, all I could think about was how much Jim loved this perky car. He loved its pick-up and the tightness of its steering. He loved the racing stripe with "Li'l Hare Racer" in flowing script. How could I tell him that our only asset, the car he had so tenderly washed and waxed—and rarely driven—was now a mangled pile of metal?

Jim's reaction was a foreshadowing of the maturity he would later use in guiding our children toward his greatest lesson, a lesson they would learn from what was now a badly twisted hunk of metal. With characteristic clarity, Jim calmed my fears. No one was injured. What else really mattered?

One large insurance check and six weeks' time saw the Rabbit refurbished right down to the beloved racing stripe. Though the body looked brand new, the patched-up motor was never the same. Still, it was ours, and we became accustomed to our vehicle's many peculiarities as we steered it through the early years of our marriage. The Rabbit saw disco and fondue, streaking and sushi, midiskirts and *Dallas* come and go.

We followed our whims to rock concerts in Atlanta and the Picasso exhibit in New York, dancing in New Orleans and beachcombing in Sanibel. Three years after the accident, our travel lust satiated, we settled down to begin our family.

Our first three children arrived in rapid succession. Jim would squeeze the three child seats into the Rabbit's backseat, kiss us good-bye and say, "Drive carefully. This car isn't much, but it's full of precious cargo."

Years went by, and after various taps and bumps, almost-missed trees and completely crushed fenders, we joked that the one original piece of metal left on the car was its top.

When the Rabbit was nine years old, we bought a van. Roomy

and pungent with that new-car smell, the Voyager had air conditioning that *worked* and electric everything. We loved it.

Each day Jim took the Rabbit to the office and left the luxury vehicle for us. The Rabbit grew shabbier and shabbier, but Jim never complained. We had a fourth child and built a home. Tuition, ballet, piano and golf lessons left little extra money for a new automobile. The horsehair in the Rabbit's seats fell out. The window handles broke off. Eventually, the driver's-side door refused to open, the seats wouldn't adjust and the clock retired permanently at 6:05. When the fenders began to rust, Li'l Hare Racer's pep gave out. Still, Jim nursed it.

One cold morning, the children and I saw him in the rain, opening the hood and tinkering with the engine to make it start, then jumping in the car and driving away.

Our culture is myopic, able to perceive only those who seem larger than life. Watching their father out in the rain that morning, our children learned about true heroes—the everyday people who struggle day to day, week to week, in constant and abiding sacrifice. Headline heroes and their splashy moments of fame pale in comparison with the extraordinary stamina of a simple but persistently selfless man.

Jim grew into a man and a father, driving that car. Every time the children and I looked at the Rabbit, we saw Jim's love and sacrifice for us. It became the symbol of all the best qualities in him. Most men's egos would not have allowed them to drive a rattletrap. Most men base their self-worth on their possessions and the image those things project. Jim cherished what we had—our health, our children, our love. He didn't worry about appearances. The more rusted the car became, the shinier Jim's halo looked to us.

When the Rabbit was 16 years old, we finally bought a new car for Jim. Surprised by the emotion I felt for our old clunker, I snapped a photograph of the Rabbit's worn and wrinkled body. Our children would remember the lessons of this car: how their father had so beautifully demonstrated what is important and what is insignificant to our lives.

We hesitated to sell the Rabbit. A participant in some of the most significant events in our lives, the little car had struggled and changed, just as we had. It was young, bright and shiny when we drove it on our honeymoon. Ailing but up to the challenge, it sputtered into Moultrie, Georgia, where we saw our first Van Gogh painting. Strong and sure, it took our family to Washington, D.C., for Fourth of July fireworks. Three times, Jim drove it ever so carefully, taking me to the hospital for our children to be born. Three times, the Rabbit safely ferried our babies back to their first homecoming. It faithfully took us to Mardi Gras and Disney World, weddings and funerals, each child to his or her first day of school.

This car had witnessed our evolution as a couple and as a family. As we drove our faithful Rabbit to the used parts lot, I looked at the faded rainbow on the rear window. We had found its pot of gold.

Jim turned off the main highway onto a dusty, rutted road. Bouncing between chain-link gates, we found ourselves surrounded by abandoned cars with no wheels, seats, doors. Jim exchanged the keys for a $50 check. I turned and walked quickly to the van, embarrassed for strangers to see my tears.

"I feel like we just dropped off the family pet to be euthanized," I said.

A smile fiddled at the corner of his mouth. He gave me a quick sideways glance. "Think of it as an organ donor," he said, accelerating through the gates. "Li'l Hare's bound to live on and on."

Leigh D. Muller

Unschooled Educator

The education of a man is never completed until he dies.

—Robert E. Lee

My dad taught me many things as I was growing up. At the time I didn't realize it, nor, I suspect, did he. Most of the lessons I learned from him were simply by association, absorbing some of his philosophy and noting how he coped with life.

Today when I hear people complain about their rough childhoods and listen to them blame their shortcomings and hardships on the lack of love and care during their formative years, I think of Dad. His childhood was very rough, but he never complained. He took responsibility for himself at a very early age.

My grandmother died when Dad was 12 years old. Why my grandfather felt he could not keep his four boys together as a family, I don't know. I do know they were quite poor because Dad once told me his only pair of shoes fell apart one winter. In order not to miss school, he wore his mother's shoes, much to the delight of his taunting classmates.

Shortly after my grandmother died, Grandfather farmed out the two older boys and sent the two younger ones to an orphanage. Working long hours on the farm, eating second at the table, and always hungry enough to relish even the bony backs and necks of chicken, my dad, at the age of 12, had to earn his room and board.

After finishing the eighth grade, Dad was forced to leave school. He simply had to make a living to support himself. Never once did I hear Dad condemn his father for not taking care of him. Never once did he complain about the hardships he suffered, alone in the world without home or family.

Since he had no family ties, Dad became what was known in those days as a "boomer." He went from town to town around Indiana and Wisconsin, staying wherever he found the best jobs. He did many things to earn his way.

He harvested crops, worked in canning factories and shoveled coal in a foundry. He even worked as an undertaker's assistant until the night he was required to go alone to a remote labor camp populated with husky, tough-looking men. Someone pointed to the body, and Dad found a big hulk of a man, brutal in appearance, who had been stabbed several times. Not one of the workers would help him load the corpse. They were afraid to touch a dead person.

That night Dad didn't stand on protocol. He didn't care whether or not he loaded the dead man into the wagon feet first, as he was supposed to do. All he wanted was to get the job done and leave as quickly as possible. After struggling with the giant body, he finally wrestled it into the wagon, then sped out of the camp as though being chased by a pack of demons. Dad was only 15 years old at the time, but that night he decided that undertaking was not the career for him.

Wherever he went, my dad never had any difficulty obtaining a job. He soon earned a reputation as a diligent and steady worker. No matter how menial the task, Dad felt you should take pride in your work. He also believed that if he were hired for an eight-hour job, he owed his employer eight hours of work. Rather than be idle if he finished the task he was doing, Dad would pick up a broom and sweep the floor or look around for something else that needed to be done. He had little tolerance for people who "goofed off" when the boss wasn't around.

By the time Dad met my mother, he was eager to settle down and have a home and family of his own. After he was married, he knew he could no longer wander from place to place seeking the best jobs, so he taught himself a trade. Dad became a machinist, and he collected the set of tools essential to that work. It always amazed me how he could measure tolerances in thousandths of an inch with his tiny micrometers. Armed with a marketable trade, Dad was able to support his family, and this he did very well.

Although Dad lacked a formal education, he impressed on my sister and me the importance of education and the joy of learning. When my sister entered college, Dad's colleagues scoffed, "Why send a girl to college? What good will that do?"

Dad would smile and say, "An education is something no one can take away from you."

"But all that money will be wasted on girls. Your daughters will just get married and have kids."

"An education is never wasted," Dad would answer calmly. "I hope my girls do get married and have children. Suppose their husbands should die, leaving them to support those children. I'd want them to make a decent living, and a good education would help them do that."

Dad said he'd seen too many widows who had to eke out a bare existence in some "greasy spoon," toiling long hours for a mere pittance; he didn't want that for his daughters. How proud my father was of my sister's and my academic achievements!

Dad accepted life without complaint. Whatever needed to be done, he did quietly and efficiently. In emergencies, he stayed calm and acted quickly. "In an emergency, use your head and your hands," was the philosophy he lived by.

It came in quite handy when I went into labor. After only 15 minutes, my son made his appearance in this world in the backseat of the car on the way to the hospital. My dad had the calm presence of mind to deliver him!

Unknowingly, Dad taught me many lessons. He helped me form my own philosophy of life. I learned never to ask "Why me?" when something unpleasant or sad occurred in my life. Dad gave me a strong work ethic and an appreciation of home and family. Because he impressed upon me the need for an education, I found that learning could enrich my life and open many doors for me.

When confronted with an emergency, I think of my Dad and try to do what he taught—use my head and my hands.

My life was blessed by a father who cared, who taught me valuable lessons and who always wanted the best for his girls.

Thanks, Dad!

Dorothy M. Reese

My Most Valuable Possession

*The events of childhood do not pass,
but repeat themselves like
seasons of the year.*

—Eleanor Farjeon

Every day when the mail carrier drops the mail into my box with a thud, I know I will find several envelopes marked "bulk mail" with my name on them. Long ago my daddy told me that "fools' names, like their faces, are always seen in public places." With his words still in mind some 80-plus years later, I can't bear the thought of my name being seen by the garbage man. So every day I spend part of the morning inking out, cutting through or tearing up these combinations of letters, printed on junk mail, that represent my most valuable possession—my name.

I learned the alphabet from the *Florida Times Union* while sitting in Papa's lap. The paper reached our house by way of his large coat pocket, along with the other afternoon mail from Jacksonville.

Most days I was swinging on the front gate waiting for him to give me a piggyback ride up the long walk leading to our big, old, white clapboard house. I would count aloud as he climbed the 10 wide steps to the porch. He plopped me down on one of the large wooden rocking chairs, hung his coat on the back of

134

another, took the newspaper out and lifted me onto his lap while he read about what had happened in the world.

One afternoon, as I played in the front yard near the gate, I felt something in my dress pocket. It was a new red crayon from my box at school. Somehow it had fallen off my desk and into my pocket.

Our yard had a white picket fence around it that had just been whitewashed. The temptation was too great. I began to scribble on one picket, just a little. The contrast between the bright red and the stark white sparked my imagination. Soon I was outside the gate, printing a letter of my name on each paling. I worked slowly and carefully. I wanted Papa to be proud of my work.

The rope swing that hung from a limb of the big oak tree was the best place to watch for him. I stood on the board seat and saw him three blocks away. I ran down the sidewalk to the corner to meet him. He hoisted me to his shoulders, held my feet and jogged to the gate.

Suddenly, he put me down. Together we surveyed my handiwork—I with extreme delight, Papa with great displeasure. Then in the sternest voice I ever heard him use, he said: "Go in the house and get a pail of water. Bring two sponges and a bar of soap so I can help you begin. When you finish this task, you will have learned a very important lesson: fools' names, like their faces, are always seen in public places." Then he added, "Your name is your most valuable possession. Be sure you treat it with respect."

Elizabeth Thomson

Few Words—Great Lessons

*Real generosity is doing something
nice for someone who'll
never find it out.*

—Frank A. Clark

I never heard my father say "I love you, Daughter." He was a product of the theory that what you do speaks more eloquently than any words you could ever utter. I never once doubted his love for me and the rest of our family. We were simple country people, living on a farm where cotton was the main crop. The work was strenuous and back-breaking; the rewards were few.

When I was five years old, my father would take cotton to be ginned and sold. A bale of cotton weighed approximately 500 pounds. I asked him about the price he had received for the cotton, and he told me they had given him five cents for it. Of course, he meant five cents per pound, but as a child I thought it was only a nickel for the whole bale.

This was during the Depression, and while things were very bad, they were not as desperate as they seemed. Even through hard times, we enjoyed our family—aunts, uncles and cousins by the dozen—our church, even our two-room school. In 1935, my father was able to purchase some farmland, and he enjoyed many productive years until his death in 1977.

He was never "political," yet he cared about his country and faithfully voted the Democratic ticket all his life. He was not called up for service in the First World War, but he saw two sons, a son-in-law, several nephews and friends answer the call from their country in World War II. It was so difficult for him to say good-bye when his sons had to return to duty after their occasional leaves that he always invented some excuse to stay away until after they had gone. Perhaps if he had been a man to share his feelings, it might have been easier for all of us.

My father always had time to go about God's business, and his testimony of faithfulness was known far and wide. Memories from my childhood include seeing him service the gasoline-powered lamps in the country church before the Rural Electricity Association came to our area. He furnished the wood for the pot-bellied heaters and assumed the responsibility of arriving early so that the church building would be warm and inviting when other worshipers arrived. He held many offices in his church until his health began to fail and he had to give them up.

He was a man of his word in the days when a handshake was as good as a signature. It was his joy to be able to accommodate anyone who was in need. He truly was a good neighbor in the biblical sense.

He passed away July 25, 1977. I was with him all day on his last day of life. I never heard him say "I love you, Daughter," but it didn't matter to me. I had a picture of his long life before me, and I could see every expression of his love for me in the things he had done.

Thank you, Daddy.

Pauline Catoe Young

Ordinary People

*People will cease to commit atrocities only
when they cease to believe absurdities.*

—Voltaire

"They were just ordinary people. People like you and me. They weren't criminals. They weren't bad people. They did nothing wrong. They were killed only because they were Jewish," my father explained to me. Over and over, he would ask, "How could it happen?" And as my father spoke these words, his eyes would well up with tears. This was my introduction to the Holocaust. My father was an American soldier during World War II. He fought in Europe and participated in the liberation of a concentration camp in Germany.

Born in Poland, my father came to the United States as a child. He believed strongly in the value of hard work, and I did not get to see him much since he worked long days. He was never there for any of my school activities or anything else I did as a child. He would often be gone before I awakened in the morning and, just as often, would return home late at night.

My father and I did share one activity: going to the synagogue on Shabbat morning. He would often fall asleep during the service, which embarrassed me, but I was happy to have the opportunity to be with him. It was on one such morning that my father told me what he had experienced during the war. When he told me what he had seen while liberating the concentration camp, I was too young to comprehend or absorb the horrors he described. I could only imagine what it must have been like for him to be Jewish and to release ordinary people, like himself, who had been imprisoned for the "crime" of being Jewish, and who had survived unspeakable horrors, barely escaping death.

My father passed away in 1976, and in the years that followed, I began to realize that his teachings had affected me in many ways. His stories of witnessing the aftermath of the Holocaust, and the unanswerable questions he raised, filled me with sadness for the suffering of others. It was through my father's stories that I perceived the pain of those who had suffered. Perhaps this was the beginning of my desire to become a psychologist—a doctor of the mind who alleviates the mental and emotional suffering that cause as much pain as physical illness.

Twenty years after my father's death, on Yom Ha-Shoah (Holocaust Memorial Day) in April 1996, my 17-year-old daughter and I took part in a memorial march from Auschwitz to Birkenau—an experience that brought my father's stories to life. I felt that I finally understood what my father had wanted to tell me when he described the liberation of the concentration camp. Now that I understand better what my father experienced, I feel closer to him—even in his absence—and to my heritage as a Jew.

Across three generations, my family and I keep the vigil he began with the simple question, "How could this happen?" I have no answer, but I will fulfill an obligation to my father by urging my son and daughter to ask that question over and over again. I will remind them of their grandfather, whose heart was full of love and pity for the innocent, ordinary people who marched to their deaths in concentration camps more than 50 years ago. Through his empathy for the nameless millions who suffered and died, my father taught me precious lessons about my identity as an indi-vidual and as part of the larger world. He helped me recognize our shared human bond, our need to be kind and good to each other. There is no greater lesson we can pass along to our children.

Joel Kimmel

Lincoln's Final Message to His Father

Good words are worth much,
and cost little.

—George Herbert

In late 1850 Lincoln's father lay dying in a farmhouse in Coles County. John Johnston—Sally's boy—wrote Lincoln semiliterate letters about Thomas's condition, saying he would not recover and wondering why Lincoln refused to reply.

"Because," Lincoln finally informed Johnston in January, 1851, "it appeared to me I could write nothing which would do any good."

And Lincoln couldn't visit his father either, since Mary was ill and he had pressing business commitments. But he did send a final message to the dying man, to that father who was a stranger to him, who perhaps hadn't been positive and close and under-standing and intelligent enough in raising his only son.

Tell him [Lincoln wrote to Johnston] to remember to call upon and confide in, our great, and good, and merciful Maker; who will not turn away from him in any extremity. He notes the fall of a sparrow, and numbers the hairs of our heads; and He will not forget the dying man, who puts his trust in Him. Say to him that if we would meet now, it is doubtful whether it would not be more painful than pleasant; but that if it be his lot to go now, he will soon have a joyous [meeting] with many loved ones gone before; and where [the rest] of us, through the help of God, hope erelong [to join] them.

On January 17, 1851, Thomas Lincoln died.

Stephen B. Oates

For My Father

What is soul? It's like electricity—
we don't really know what it is, but it's
a force that can light a room.

—Ray Charles

A physician is, or at least is supposed to be, fully versed in handling the professional, social and even spiritual aspects of death. But the sudden death of my father last year made bare the facets of this phenomenon to which I was oblivious before. I was overwhelmed by apprehensions, regrets and grief that no professional expertise could eradicate or ease. My father's presence, his advice, his prayers were an invincible shield between me and all adversity, and because of it I fearlessly took on every challenge that came my way. After his death, there quietly appeared a strange reluctance, a caution in my approach.

In Whittemore's words,

> With his passing I was abruptly stripped of any illusions of my own immortality; no longer might I comfort myself with the thought that he was next in line ahead of me. For any boy, that is one of his father's silent functions—to stand as a shield between his son and the abyss.

My first impression of my father is that of a stranger in uniform standing in our doorway. It was the time of World War II, and he

had volunteered to serve. Soon after the war, he agreed to lead
an expedition to take over a military post for our country in the
snowy mountains of Kashgar. By the time he came home, I was
already five. Our relationship began with my having this odd feeling of strangeness about him, but his noninsistent and gentle
approach gradually reassured me. What really made me comfortable was my child's eye keenly noticing how those who met my
father even in the street greeted him with respect and a smile.

Nor was discipline lacking in his parenting. I was a handful in
my teens, and had it not been for proper disciplining, I surely
would have neglected my studies. A mulberry tree stood next to
our house, and occasionally my father had to resort to the use of
one of its branches to set me right. After my graduation from
medical school, whenever I and my father walked by that tree,
we would look at each other and burst out laughing. My childhood friends still joke that were it not for that mulberry tree, I
wouldn't be a doctor today.

My father also was the role model in my professional conduct.
His utter lack of greed and his intense concern for his patients
nurtured in me the desire to become a scrupulous physician. He
was fiercely self-dependent and would rather limit his needs than
be under obligation to others. This taught me the true meaning
and value of self-respect. For years, when I still was a boy in
school, it was my father's routine to play chess each evening with
the Nawab of Kalabagh (in Pakistan). When later the Nawab
became the governor of our state, I, at the prodding of my
friends, thoughtlessly asked my father if he would get me an
appropriate medical posting from the governor.

"No, Son," he made it emphatically clear, "if I do this, all my
friends will think I foster relationships for personal gain. The quick-
est way to lose respect in the eyes of others is to bring them your
needs." I can still hear him saying, "Faith in God and self-reliance
mean that the need you cannot meet yourself isn't your need."

Yet, when it came to others, I don't remember him ever saying
no to anyone who sought his help. Many times I saw him knocking on the office door of even the lowliest of bureaucrats to plead
for a job for some poor family man. Many of his patients were

country people who traveled miles to seek his help. He gave them free medicine, and when any of them needed longer care, he put them up in a spare room attached to our home. In those days there weren't many hospitals. My mother looked after their meals and other needs, and when they were ready to go home, my father bought their train or bus tickets. This happened so often that for a long time I thought it was a required part of medical practice. His death took away from the people around him an ever-willing benefactor; from me, my earthly wellspring of guidance and steadfastness.

Despite his weaknesses—he was a pitiful money manager and a chain smoker till his last day—I gradually came to believe that if he set his heart to it, there wasn't a thing in the world he couldn't take care of. This belief in the goodness and greatness of this man whom everyone admired had coated my subconscious with an impervious layer of security, which his death suddenly peeled away. Even throughout my adult life, I felt greatly reassured after consulting my father. My confidence in his wisdom, experience and sincerity was so deep-seated that I never felt even the slightest embarrassment when he drew my attention to some silly flaw in my reasoning or approach to a problem.

My apprehensions upon his loss arose from my losing his guidance that, in my mind, never missed its mark, my regrets from not having been there with him all that time, my grief from losing someone who loved me so dearly yet so selflessly. The thought of to whom I would now open myself when plagued by fears and doubts relentlessly gnawed on my mind. Because my father's wisdom and experience are there no more to boost me, a more deliberate behavior has quietly displaced the impetuosity in me. A keener awareness of my own mortality brought on by his passing has erased from my mind every temptation to place any expedient consideration before honesty or self-esteem. Becoming reft of his support has induced me to rely subconsciously on what he imparted to my character.

As the shock of my father's death began to wear off, my attention became more focused on my own role as the leading link in the life chain of my family. I now realize more acutely that the good that my father had must now live through me. I came to see that for a son, the son-father relationship is an honorable debt that when paid honestly perpetuates happiness. The question of how one pays a dead father the debt one owes has brought to my view the flip side of life's coin, revealing that one pays to one's children the debt one owes to one's father. That is how good is passed on from one generation to the next. I found in me an unconstrained willingness to be more attentive to the needs of my children, more eager to extend to them my hand in help and more tolerant to their youthful antics.

I am also almost imperceptibly acquiring a demeanor with my patients that was so characteristic of my father. Where I used to feel strain on hearing the clinically unnecessary and repetitious details some patients have the habit of giving, I now find myself much more willing to listen. I have become more forbearing with the excuses my patients bring me and, like my father, I also try to extend nonprofessional assistance to those who need it. But such good has its own reward. No amount of money and no amount of hard work can bring the kind of happiness I felt when I drove home an elderly patient whose ride had left him stranded in my office.

Even in his death, my father has taught me how to be a better father and a better man. An intelligent person would learn from anyone's death.

To ponder the philosophical and spiritual perceptions of death is an efficient balm to the bereaved's grief and depression. This is not necessarily restricted to one's religious beliefs, for a rational analysis of day-to-day observations on life and death may also bring solace by imparting a clearer understanding of this reality. Death is not the end. Socrates, though not very vocal about God, was totally convinced of the immortality of the soul. Hence, when authorities hand Socrates the cup of hemlock, Crito asks him in Plato's *Phaedo*, "How shall we bury you?"

"However you please, if you can catch me, and I do not get away from you," replies Socrates with a gentle laugh.

Clearly, he was speaking of one's true self, his soul, which on leaving the prison of flesh becomes free of all confines and never perishes. Death is a transformation. Faith is an indispensable source of comfort and courage when material means fail us. Day after day in our professional practice, we see the comfort that turning to faith brings to patients with diseases that have reached beyond our ability to treat. Both faith and reason helped me overcome my irreplaceable loss and made me a better human in the process.

Yes, my father is dead, but his existence has not ended. He continues to live in heaven, in reality and in our hearts symbolically. I am sad no more. My bosom is still full of his love, my deeds still add to his good name and my prayers are still filled with supplications for his salvation. And I add to my every prayer, "Bless too, O Almighty, all the caring fathers, those living with us on this earth and those living with God's promise in the hereafter."

Khalid J. Awan

A Temperate Man

No mind is thoroughly well organized that is deficient in a sense of humor.

—Samuel Taylor Coleridge

My father was the best man I have ever known. He was born in 1901. He lived through some very good times and some very bad times.

When I was 12, Daddy developed tuberculosis. The year was 1936, and he was confined in a sanitarium for tuberculosis patients. The sanitarium was located in a small town in southern Mississippi, about 60 miles from our home. These were Depression years, and looking back I can only imagine how frightening those years must have been for both my father and my mother.

Fortunately, we had a large, loving family. My father, mother and I had lived with my father's uncle since I was a baby. Uncle Willard had lived alone in the big antebellum house where my great-grandparents had lived and where he had grown up. He had never married, so we were his family, and he was ours.

Mama and I, together with other members of our family, went to visit Daddy every weekend. The trips were hard. There was very little money for gasoline for the car. Worse still, the roads we traveled to reach the sanitarium were not paved, and "air conditioning" were words we had never heard. The dust from the gravel

roads was so stifling that we wore large handkerchiefs tied around
our heads like masks. We probably looked like a car full of bandits.

I wrote a poem about my dad while he was in the sanitarium
to let him know I missed and loved him. I have the original copy,
which I had mailed to him in 1936. I found it among some papers
he had kept in a safe place throughout his life. Although he died
in 1979, it was not until 1989 that I finally had the courage to go
through the things he had kept in a brown leather folder.

Among other things, there were letters from his mother and
father written to him when he was in business school in New
Orleans, a lovely picture of my mother when she was young and
this handwritten poem from me:

MY DAD

He's the best man in this town
To me he's a man of great renown
He very seldom wears a frown,
   My Dad
He's the one who knows what's best
He always says, "That's a beautiful dress"
I always ask God to bless
   My Dad
I have to go many a mile
To get to see him once in a while,
But when I see him, he's wearing a smile,
   My Dad
He even loves me when I'm bad
Or even when I'm very mad
I bet that everyone wishes they had
   My Dad

My father was released from the sanitarium after a full year,
and our life returned to what could be considered nearly normal,
under the circumstances. His illness and the Depression did cause
hardship for our family. Daddy, however, never felt sorry for himself or let life get him down. His Christian faith was the sustaining force of his entire life.

If I had to sum up what I learned from my father in one word, it would be *temperance*—moderation in all things, not abstinence. My father loved life: people, music, laughter and family. And people of all ages, shapes and sizes loved him. The Presbyterian minister who conducted his funeral became so emotional that he had to stop his eulogy and compose himself in order to finish the service.

Daddy played tennis, golf, bridge and poker. He loved the horse races in New Orleans, Louis Armstrong, Dixieland Jazz, Jack Benny, the Marx Brothers and Guy Lombardo. He loved entertaining and being entertained.

When I was about five years old, and he and Mother were in their late 20s, I remember a party they had. They were going to a dance at the country club and were having an intermission party at our home. I had been asleep in my room, but the laughter woke me when they and their friends arrived for the party. I remember thinking how glamorous it was to be grown up, wearing such pretty clothes, dancing and having a party.

My father was a dedicated Christian and told me often that he did some of his best witnessing at cocktail parties. In terms of money, he gave far more than a tithe to the church. Mother had told me that Dad took his Bible on their honeymoon, and that they had knelt and prayed together that their marriage would be blessed. And it was—until he died, 56 years later.

After his death, my brother and I found a book in which he had kept a record of all his betting gains and losses. I'm glad he was a temperate man. He was a good accountant, but a poor gambler.

Dad made home-brewed beer during Prohibition. It wasn't legal, but in the legally dry state of Mississippi—where an official was designated to collect a black-market tax on liquor—I think the point is moot.

My father was a very outgoing "people person." He loved visiting and talking to both friends and strangers. Once he started, he couldn't stop. One thing would remind him of something else, and he would tell a story that reminded him of another story, which reminded him of another story, and on and on he went.

Mama, who was frustrated with his tales, shouted at him one day as he rambled on, "Why can't you be like your son and say what you have to say in 10 words or less?"

She would rue the day she ever uttered those words because the next day when Daddy came home for lunch, she asked, as she did every day, "What's the news in town today?" Daddy very slowly and deliberately said, "Bob Brady had a seizure at the post office and . . ." With that, he turned and walked out of the room. After that, no one dared interrupt him again.

Long, rambling stories are a genetic inheritance, but so are many other traits I inherited from my father for which I am grateful. Not the least of these is a love of people.

Looking back at my life of over 70 years, I am grateful to my father for all the reasons I have enumerated. I am grateful that he taught me not to let life get me down. I am grateful he had a sense of humor and that he taught me how to laugh at myself. I am grateful he demonstrated for me exactly what temperance meant.

Betsy Bee

While My Son Was in School, I Learned . . .

The most important thing that parents can teach their children is how to get along without them.

—Frank A. Clark

On Saturday we reach a milestone that many parents eagerly anticipate: we get to watch our son walk across the stage at his college graduation.

Actually, he finished at midterm. But after four and a half years at The Citadel—the military college of South Carolina—there's no way we're going to miss seeing him walk the walk. We think that he wants to do it, too, but he may be only humoring us.

I was recently asked to speak to a group of parents who are about to become empty-nesters. I was invited perhaps because we've survived the trials of college, but more likely it's because I was the only one who said yes. (Early college training myself: never turn down a free meal.)

I found myself struggling to find something significant to say to people who are about to learn whether they can still hold adult conversations with each other. Preparing for the talk sent me to

Reprint courtesy of the *Fort Worth Star-Telegram*.

the computer to reread letters to my son during his college career—many of them written while he was in basic training at Fort Benning, Georgia, as part of his enlistment in the South Carolina National Guard.

And I am reminded of lessons that he taught us.

There was the day that the whole family accompanied him to the infirmary so doctors could determine whether his broken hand had healed enough so they could make him do hundreds of push-ups. He noted he was the only cadet with his entire family present.

We learned that even when your child is in college, you still have the most significant power that parents possess: you can embarrass the heck out of him.

The next summer was basic training, a neat experience for a kid, we thought. Then the speaker at his graduation reminded us: "The mission of the infantry is to close with the enemy and take him prisoner or kill him."

And that taught us that children grow up and do very adult things and that you never get to quit worrying about your children, college or no. (One benefit: when they're in college, you don't always know when you should be worried.)

Other lessons followed:

- You can't do much to pick your child's friends or future spouse. All you can do is hope that common sense and previous training kick in somewhere along with the hormones.
- Even when your child is in college, you find that you can't keep silent about the important things in life (this prompted by a letter about the dangers of alcohol usage at school). But lectures delivered to an adult child are different from lectures delivered to a child child.
- Although college students are adults in almost every sense of the word, they are adults-in-training, and still need guidance and advice from their parents. The hard part is figuring out when to say something and when to keep your mouth shut.

As I read back over the letters to my son—there aren't as many as there should have been because we generally talked on the telephone (the telephone bill is another coming shock for parents of college students)—one particular paragraph jumps out at me:

> We are, as I tell you in almost every letter, proud of you. We like your attitude toward life, we like your temperament, we like your sense of humor, and we like the way you go about selecting friends.

And the lesson? Being a parent doesn't change much just because the child is a thousand miles away.

Paul K. Harral

My Father's Advice

*I have found the best way
to give advice to your children is to
find out what they want and then
advise them to do it.*

—Harry S. Truman

I was 23 and about to set off for Europe. I'd been saving since college, living at home to cut expenses. Now I planned to quit my job and travel as long as my money lasted.

A few days before my departure, my father handed me a handwritten sheet of paper. "Norman, here are some things I want you to keep in mind."

Surprised, I took the paper to my room. Dad wasn't one for writing.

The sheet was headed "reminders," and there were 29. The first few were sensible enough:

"Check in with the U.S. embassy in each country."

"Keep change in your pockets."

"Put money under your pillow at night."

Then came, as I knew it would, the advice meant to cramp my style:

Reprinted with permission from the September 1990 *Reader's Digest*. ©1990 by The Reader's Digest Assn., Inc.

"Don't pick up strange girls. You may be sorry."
"Don't climb mountains. You might get hurt."
"Don't hitchhike."
"Don't get tattooed."
It was always that way with Dad, a drumbeat of do's and don'ts from morning to night. There was never an easy conversation with him. Always, it was Dad telling me what to think, what to do, what dangers to avoid. As a teenager I decided he had dedicated his life to stamping out my fun and freedom.

That's not the way he'd lived *his* adolescence, though.

Charles Wesson Smith was born in a small town in Kentucky, one of six children of the general-store owner. He hadn't finished high school when he left town by hopping a freight train.

My mother, a Texan, met my father when both lived in Oklahoma City, she working in a bank, he as a salesman. What first attracted her was his voice: deep, rich, confident and spiced with country expressions. "You did your best," he'd say, "that's all a mule can do."

After they married, my parents traveled the United States, moving whenever the mood struck. My father could always find something to sell. They were in Texas during the big oil strikes, in Hollywood in the era of the great movie studios, in New York for the 1939 World's Fair. Not until my brother Jim was born did they settle down and buy their first house. By the time I came along two years later, they had left their adventuring days behind.

I remember Dad driving us to school, giving the same lecture every morning: "Boys, you're getting the tools of your trade. Get them now or you'll be like a carpenter without his tools—you won't be able to make a living."

The lecture never inspired me to do much learning. I day-dreamed my way through classes. In the schoolyard I was in a lot of fights. That stemmed from Dad's advice: "Give bullies a good fight, and they won't bother you anymore."

It didn't work out exactly that way. Kids my age quit harassing me, but when word got out that the little kid in the second grade wouldn't run, the fourth-grade bullies sought me out. I followed Dad's advice even when I realized it had a flaw because I knew he wouldn't run from a fight himself. And I wanted him to be proud of me.

As I grew older, however, I began to resent Dad's counseling. I rebelled not only against his advice but against his beliefs, too. I never rejected him personally, however. And for that I'm thankful, for he died suddenly when I was in my mid-20s.

Years later when my son, Eric, was born, I pondered what I wanted to teach him. Only then did it dawn on me just how much I'd been taught by my father. I had learned the way children always learn—not by words but by example.

Dad's most important lessons were ones he never verbalized. I have tried to put them into words.

A man's main job is to take care of the people who depend on him. Dad did this in the old-fashioned way. He worked hard to pay for everything we needed. He took care of my mother's family, too—Virgiebelle and her daughter, Dodie.

Once, Virgiebelle phoned my mother, extremely agitated. Her ex-husband, Ray, she reported, was acting crazy again. He'd taken Dodie, then four, and said he wasn't going to give her back. My father said he'd take care of it. He went to Ray's hotel, knowing he wouldn't have much standing with the law if trouble arose; he'd be the uncle-in-law kidnapping a child from her own father. But Dad was a salesman, and he knew men's weaknesses.

He brought a bottle of bourbon and said, "Ray, we've got to talk, so let's have a drink first." My father could outdrink most men then, and he soon had Dodie back with her mother.

Virgiebelle and Dodie lived with us for the first five years of my life. When they moved into their own home, I couldn't understand it. But years later, when my mother's cousin, Marianne, came to stay with us for a few months because she was "having problems," I was old enough to realize not every man welcomed in-laws into his house.

Never boast, never pretend, never say anything that isn't true. My father's world, that of commission salesmen, was filled with big talkers. They'd often come by the house. Many had worked for my father and were looking for an "advance." Dad was an easy touch.

I remember one salesman spinning visions of fortunes to be

made with a new deal he wanted my father to take on. "It can't miss, Charlie!" he said.

When I asked my father about it afterward, he just smiled. "Everybody in this business has a sure thing," he said.

I often heard my father's sales pitches; he'd work the phone in the evening. But I never heard him make the kind of claims the big talkers made. He never said anything he didn't believe himself. And he never bothered to instruct me about telling the truth. I don't think it occurred to him that it was something a father had to do.

Share with the less fortunate. Once when Dad was home working while the rest of us were at our summer house, he wrote my mother: "When I came home last night, Anna's little girl was vitally interested in Norman's bicycle, and I gave it to her." Anna was our longtime mother's helper. Though Dad did replace my bike, I thought he had no right to give it away. Not until years later could I appreciate the charm of that kind of spontaneous giving.

When you say you're going to do something, do it. Some childhood memories are engraved in a way you know will never fade. One of mine occurred when I was barely four. My father was unconscious on the kitchen floor. He had passed out from drinking too much. Jim had his right arm, and I had his left as we tried to drag him to the living room couch.

I don't remember what happened next. Probably my mother came downstairs. But not long afterward, my father joined AA. He said he wasn't going to touch alcohol again. And he never did. I didn't then understand the powerful hold alcohol could have, but I did understand, growing up, that my mother never worried about my father's falling off the wagon. He'd said he wasn't going to drink anymore, and that was that.

When you're right, don't quit. One day in my high-school freshman year, Dad picked Jim and me up from school. "You'd better read this before you hear it from someone else," he said, handing us a newspaper.

"D.A. Nabs Mail Fraud Crooks" declared the headline above my father's picture.

Dad calmly explained that he'd done nothing wrong, but

complaints had been filed against some salesmen, and an ambitious district attorney decided to make a fuss. Since Dad was the biggest fish in the pond, they arrested him. But we weren't to worry. It would blow over quickly—there was no case.

I did worry. Not about Dad—he'd be all right—but about classmates saying something. When they didn't, I stopped worrying.

But then my father was indicted. He could have pleaded guilty and settled for a minimal fine, but Dad was innocent. Even if it meant risking jail, he'd never say he'd been dishonest. The trial took a long time. He paid a fortune to lawyers, his business was ruined, but in the end Dad was found not guilty.

Though innocent of crime, my father was seriously guilty of misjudgment. I can remember the dinner-table conversations that presaged his indictment.

"Charles," my mother would say, "you know Frank is trouble."

"I know, Genevieve, but he deserves a second chance."

Frank was Dad's oldest friend, a fellow salesman. I knew him as a big man who drove a pink Cadillac and told great stories. He'd gotten in trouble with the law, blamed it on alcohol and said he needed my father's help.

Dad cut him in on some franchise sales he was handling. He separated his dealings from Frank's, but when Frank reverted to his slippery sales techniques, Dad was inevitably dragged in. Frank was tried separately from my father and convicted.

Don't turn your back on friends who are down and out. When Frank got out of prison, Dad took him in. Frank paid his keep by entertaining us. Even my mother laughed at his tales of tending the prison's sheep.

Dad was softhearted but no fool. After a few months, when Frank had made no progress in getting a job, Dad checked the basement bar. Bottles had been replaced empty or watered. Frank was soon gone from our lives. A year later I saw his picture in the post office. He was now wanted for hijacking.

It was good he was gone because a friend of my brother, who had family troubles, was coming to live with us, at Dad's invitation.

It does no good to complain. My father was always being operated on: kidney stones, hernia, prostate, skin cancer. I remember visiting him after surgery, aware that the latest complication had just about done him in, dismayed at how feeble he was. Yet he never complained, even in severe pain. The only definitive comment I recall, whispered from his hospital bed: "Well, boys, that was a close one."

He was far from a saint. He could be plunged into black moods by his sieges of bad health, economic reverses and legal battles. In many ways, it could be said, life wasn't fair to him. But he didn't expect it to be, so he uttered no complaints.

Talk with your children. I was living in New York when my father called. He was working in the city and suggested we meet for dinner. I knew a German restaurant I figured he'd like and was pleased to be able to recommend it.

But more pleasing and surprising to me was the way dinner went. For once he didn't spend the whole time giving advice I didn't want. He talked *with* me.

I walked him to the bus terminal. While we waited, he leaned on the railing over the main lobby. My father had once been a thick-bodied six-footer. Now I saw how thin and shrunken he was. He then told me something that astonished me. He said he still felt, inside his head, like a young man and couldn't believe he'd passed 60.

"You don't know, at your age, how fast time goes," he said. He paused and then added: "If I never really talked with you boys as much as I'd have liked to, it was because there was so little time and so much I had to teach you. I just didn't want you to make all the mistakes I made. I wanted to save you from some of the troubles I had."

I wanted to say, "Thank you, Dad, for telling me that." I knew at last I was a man to my father. We could talk with each other. But I was too enthralled by the evening to say what I was feeling.

It was the last conversation we ever had.

I was in Florida on a business trip when I called home. Virgiebelle was there with my mother. Dad had had a stroke the previous night, after coming home from work. He'd always said he wanted to work till the day he died. He got his wish. My wish, for another talk with my father, would go unfulfilled.

I now know things I didn't know when my father was alive. Time does go awfully fast. There is so much to teach my boy and so little time; I've watched him change from baby to child to boy in less time certainly than I took. I know the temptation always to be telling him things, the things he'll need to survive, to be a good person.

But I remember my father's final lesson. My boy will learn by what I am and what I do far more than by what I tell him.

So when Eric, age eight, says, "Dad, can we talk?" I put down my book and say, "Sure." I think for a second he wants my advice about something, but then I remember.

He doesn't want advice. He just wants to talk.

Norman Lewis Smith

A Tough Act to Follow

Cecile Barnett received the following letter from her son, Mike, after her husband's death. Widowed after 51 years of marriage to a man "who did not have a mean streak in his body," she is grateful for the love and devotion of her children and grandchildren.

May 18, 1993

Mother, Mother, Mother:

Before you read this letter, get yourself some Puffs because I am sure you will cry (and laugh) as much as I did while writing this letter.

At the airport, as Phyllis and I were leaving, you said that I should be proud of the man I am. I thank you very much for that compliment. I will tell you this: I would not be 10 percent the man I am now if it weren't for you and Pop. There is no way I can possibly thank you enough for all of the energy, guidance, direction and attention that you put forth to help make my life what it is today.

Dad was my father, my partner and my best friend. He was unbelievable. He was the most incredible role model any son, or for that matter, any human being, could ever have. Dad was the type of role model anyone could respect and learn from.

Dad lived better and died better than anyone I know. His entire life is what Hollywood dreamed of. All of the TV shows like *Father Knows Best* that portray ideal families were probably written with you and Dad in mind. I hope and pray that when I die I have done enough good to get to connect with Dad and you

161

again. Bill Barnett is a very tough act to follow. But I can do it, and I will do it. You can bet on it.

Throughout my life, both Dad and you have been there to support my every move and decision. When I made the wrong decisions and had to suffer the consequences, both of you were there to help me out of my predicaments. You never rubbed my nose in the mess I had made or told me I was wrong. Instead, you would help me search for the lessons in the error, the silver lining in the dark cloud.

Both you and Dad taught me to respect every living thing, regardless of color, race or creed. You taught me to place others' interests first, and to make sure that everyone around me was treated fairly. You taught me that the short end of the stick can hit the ball just as far, and sometimes farther.

Dozens and dozens of friends surround us in this time of need. Don't kid yourself—they hurt just as much as we do. Dad not only touched the hearts and minds of others, but also had an incredible impact on their lives. Everyone misses Dad. Everyone cries when hearing of this great loss. And why not? He was one of the best men ever to walk the earth. To think—he was my father, Johanna's father, your husband, and best friend to us all! We are extremely lucky to have had that privilege.

When I remember my times with Dad, I can only recollect straightforward, honest communications. There was no beating around the bush. Dad always insisted on the truth. White lies were not acceptable; fibs were not acceptable. Today, when I look at the success I have, I believe it is because of the virtues he instilled in me.

When I returned home, one of my close friends asked me what I considered to be the most important thing I learned from Dad. I could not answer then because there were so many things he taught me. I will try now: Dad taught me to enjoy life and to treat life with respect, integrity, justice and decency.

I hope I can live up to his example.

Forever yours,
your best and only son,
Michael Barnett

Contributors

Betsy Bee recently retired from her position in the executive office of the governor of Florida, where her employment spanned 10 years and 3 governors. Now launching a second career as a writer, she is currently working on a collection of essays and stories recalling her life as a Mississippi "Southern belle."

Christine E. Belleris is the editorial director of Health Communications, Inc., and a freelance writer. Prior to her career in book publishing, she was a legislative aide/assistant press secretary in the Washington, D.C., office of U.S. Congressman Ken Kramer. A native of Denver, Colorado, she is a graduate of the University of Colorado at Boulder. She and her husband, Jeff, have since traded the snow-capped Rockies for the sandy beaches of Boca Raton, Florida. When she's not buried in paperwork, Christine enjoys racewalking, bicycling, traveling and reading.

Winnifred Comfort is a native Californian and the mother of two daughters, Alisa and Janelle. Active in aquatics for many years, she has been a physical education and movement specialist for children, and currently teaches water fitness to adults. She has been featured in five major aquatic company instructional and product videos.

Virginea Dunn Cooper describes herself as a "genuine Florida Cracker," born in Titusville, Florida. For the past 25 years, she has been in charge of the Lafayette Park Writers Workshop in Tallahassee. A writer whose work has been published in various magazines and in the *Washington Star,* she is inclined to nonfiction and poetry, which she says "comes naturally."

Harry C. Copeland, of Norcross, Georgia, has had a diverse career as a teacher, social worker and business consultant. With two degrees in journalism from Florida State University, he has been a prolific writer of feature articles and columns that have appeared in newspapers and regional magazines, including the *Dothan [Alabama] Eagle, Panama City Today* and the *Journalism Quarterly.*

Jennifer Engemann was born in Kalamazoo, Michigan, and now resides in Pittsburgh, Pennsylvania. A poet and playwright, her play *Fathers Not There* was featured at the 1993 National Conference on Child Abuse and Neglect. Most recently, she and her husband published *Glimpses,* a collection of poetry about neighbors and friends she has met along the way.

Barbara B. Griffin hails from Tallahassee, Florida, where she writes stories and essays amid a busy life as the grandmother of 6 and great-grandmother of 13.

Ralph Keyes, of Yellow Springs, Ohio, is the editor of *Sons on Fathers: A Book of Men's Writing*, a collection that explores how sons come to terms with their fathers, published by HarperCollins.

Joel Kimmel has been a licensed psychologist in Coral Springs, Florida, for the past 18 years. In addition to his private practice, Dr. Kimmel serves as a psychological consultant to a number of corporations on issues including workplace violence, health promotion and employee conflict resolution.

Mary B. Ledford is a wife, mother, grandmother and retired registered nurse. She wrote her first prize-winning essay at 12 years of age. She has written three books about her heritage and childhood as gifts for her children, Susan and Tom, and her four grandchildren. She is currently at work on a novel. She and her husband, Pat, reside in historic Jonesborough, Tennessee, in the foothills of the Great Smoky Mountains.

Michael Levy, of New York City, affirms that necessity is the father of invention. He is writing stories that help parents survive their children's bedtime hour. For the big children, he's developing *A Bridge over Troubled Thoughts*, essays about life's challenges. He thanks God for his wife, Chavi, and their children, Tehilah and Aharon.

Patsy P. Lewis, author and illustrator, has written moving stories of growing up on a farm in South Carolina in her book *Barefoot-n-Cotton*, which she dedicated to her father, Edmund A. Payne, and from which the story "A Leather-Necked Farmer" is excerpted. Her career has included rearing two children, John and Elizabeth; heading the chamber of commerce in Helen, Georgia; serving as director of the Carolina Framing School in Charlotte, North Carolina; and owning Frames and Calico in Camden, South Carolina, where she exhibited and sold the work of numerous artists.

Laura Marshall is a quilter who would rather create stories with fabric than with words but thoroughly enjoyed writing "My Father's Voice." She is the daughter of Margo Marshall-Olmstead and the late Robert Marshall, and she resides in Tallahassee, Florida, with her husband and two children.

Margo Marshall-Olmstead is a native of Scotland who currently resides in Tallahassee, Florida, where her life revolves around writing poetry and essays and her role as mother of 7, grandmother of 17, and great-grandmother of 8. Her book of poetry, *Six-Pence Worth of Dreams*, was published in 1970.

George Eyre Masters was born in Philadelphia, Pennsylvania, raised in Lima, Peru, educated at Georgetown University in Washington, D.C., and now makes his home in San Francisco, California. Over the past 25 years, his work has been published in *Reader's Digest, Yachting Magazine,* the *San Francisco Chronicle* and the *Denver Post.* He is at work on a novel entitled *The Salt Tattoo,* based on his voyage across the North Pacific aboard a cargo ship.

Jane Mayes is a retired teacher and high school librarian. She lives in Port Austin on the tip of Michigan's "Thumb," where she and her husband raise standardbred harness horses. Her poems have appeared in two anthologies as well as in national magazines, and she writes a weekly column for the *Port Austin Times.*

Leigh D. Muller resides in Tallahassee, Florida, and has been a member of the Lafayette Park Writers Group for the past four years.

Dorothy M. Reese is a former English teacher whose fiction and nonfiction has been published in several national publications. She is a member of the Tallahassee Writers Guild and is at work on a young-adult novel based on the true story of a young woman who posed as a man during the Revolutionary War.

Dorothy C. Rose is a teacher at Daniel Boone High School in Gray, Tennessee. She lives with her brother, William Lee Carter, on a farm in Johnson City, Tennessee. She is the mother of three grown sons, David, Duane and Dale Rose, and the proud grandmother of Devin.

Mo-Shuet Tam, born, raised and educated in Hong Kong, did graduate work on a British Commonwealth Scholarship in Edinburgh and London, where she earned her postgraduate diploma and Ph.D. in general linguistics. She teaches at City College in San Francisco, where she is recognized as a "teacher who makes a difference," and is coordinator of the English as a Second Language program.

Elizabeth Thomson, affectionately known as "Miss T," taught at Florida State University for many years. After her retirement, she joined the Writers Workshop in Tallahassee. Her essays and stories have been published in the *Christian Science Monitor* and other national publications.

Laurel Turner lives in the Cascade foothills of central Washington state, where she is a wife and the mother of three sons. As a construction claims analyst, her work requires a great deal of travel and technical writing, but her favorite pastime is writing tributes to those she holds most dear—her family.

Gale A. Workman is a journalism professor at Florida A&M University in Tallahassee. She was a newspaper journalist for 12 years prior to earning her Ph.D. in higher education.

Bettie B. Youngs, Ph.D., Ed.D., is an international lecturer and the author of 14 books published in 30 languages, including *Values from the Heartland: Stories of an American Farmgirl* (from which "The Pheasant" is excerpted) and *Gifts of the Heart: Stories That Celebrate Life's Defining Moments*. Contact: Bettie B. Youngs, 3060 Racetrack View Dr., #101-109, Del Mar, CA 92014.

THE
Chicken Soup for the Soul Series
PRESENTS

Chicken Soup for the Soul™

The *New York Times* bestselling sensation that started the *Chicken Soup* phenomenon. Here are the original 101 stories that continue to capture the hearts and imaginations of millions. #262X—$12.95

A 2nd Helping of Chicken Soup for the Soul™

You'll find more hope, joy and inspiration in this sequel to the award-winning bestseller, *Chicken Soup for the Soul.* This collection of 101 stories will leave you feeling good about yourself and the world around you. #3316—$12.95

A 3rd Serving of Chicken Soup for the Soul™

Nourish your heart, mind and soul with this new collection of stories and reflections. Each will encourage you to live more passionately, love more unconditionally and seize your dreams with determination. #3790—$12.95

A 4th Course of Chicken Soup for the Soul™

This batch brings you 101 exceptional stories, tales and verses guaranteed to lift your spirits, soothe your soul and warm your heart. #4592—$12.95

Selected books are available in hardcover, large print, audiocassette and compact disc.

Available in bookstores everywhere or call **1-800-441-5569** for Visa or MasterCard orders. Prices do not include shipping and handling.

Your response code is **BKS**.